I Am

Enough

In Christ

Please excuse my imperfections
I'm not a final copy.
Be encouraged!

I Am Enough In Christ

Copyright © 2019 by Infinitely More Life Publishing
Published by Infinitely More Life Publishing
P.O. Box 510376 New Berlin, WI 53151
ISBN 978-0-9859456-3-3

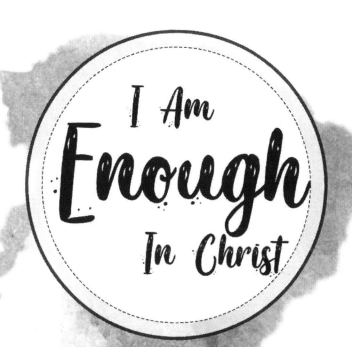

Table Of Contents

DEDICATION

This book is dedicated to all the people that have taught me to live in what Christ says I am, not what I think.

Pat Molitor, who first taught me how to read the Bible and walked me through the difficult times in the early years. Erica Berres, for being a living example of living like Christ.

Nicole Atieno and many other Kenyan friends who taught me how to live for Christ when life is very hard.

Beth Moore, Joyce Meyer, Henry Blackby, for their impactful books and Bible studies.

Even more than those in the past, this book is dedicated to YOU---the reader, who is eager to know more about who you are in Christ and live in that! Welcome! This book is for you!

No matter what you have done – drugs, abortion, divorce, financial missteps, bad decisions. No matter what has been done to you – sexual abuse, rape, physical abuse, abandonment. God loves you just the way you are right now! He will never love you any more or less than at this very moment. He IS NOT looking for you to perform, shape up on your own, or pretend you have it all together. In fact, He enjoys you even more because of your weaknesses. They cause you to rely on Him, not yourself.

All He wants from you is to seek Him for your answers. Don't seek more stuff. Don't seek the phone to complain and talk. Don't seek food, alcohol, TV binging, or anything else when you are stressed.

As you turn to Him and seek Him, He will lead, guide and direct you in life and purpose, you will find the JOY that you are meant to live in.

Take it from a control freak, Many of the above references come from my own life story. Fear, anxiety, and depression ruled my life for many years. There is freedom available and that freedom is found in Jesus through His word, prayer, and knowing that "I Am Enough In Christ." My life is a testimony to that. Yours can be, too!

Love,

Carrie Reichartz

Founder of Infinitely More Life &
Compiler/Producer of the I Am Enough In Christ Book

Strength: Abundant Life Is Yours!

BY CHOU HALLEGRA

"The thief comes only to steal and kill and destroy;
I have come that they may have life, and have it to the full."
(John 10:10 New International Version)

I had read John 10:10 many times in my life. While I knew it to be true (and I still believe it to be true) somehow, I did not see it, or feel it, in my life. What was this Abundant Life that Christ was speaking about?

Early in my faith, I might have not known what the abundant life looked like, but whatever it was, I knew I wasn't living it. Depressed, anxious, worn out, put down and let down – my life felt like a never-ending nightmare. Every morning, I was crowned the Queen of Survival.

I was sick and tired of living in survival mode and wanted the misery to be over. My kids needed me, I thought - so I struggled through day by day while I waited for my last day. I fearfully contemplated the cost of living and the cost of dying, wondering how and why my life did not reflect abundance. These questions bounced around in my head, day in and day out, for what seemed like forever. I then examined the Scriptures and discovered certain truths that changed my life.

4

*Instead of clinging to God when life is hard,
the devil wants us to walk away from our ever-present source of strength,
God Himself. Don't let him do that to you.*

The devil is on a mission and it's not for our good.

The first part of John 10:10 says, "The thief comes only to steal and kill and destroy..." This tells me that it's not God's will to destroy things in my life. God only targets sin for destruction and once that is taken down, He seeks to make things more beautiful. We see the same concept in 2 Corinthians 5:17: "Therefore, if anyone is in Christ, the new creation has come: The old has gone, the new is here!" When we come to Christ, He destroys the old so we can have a clean slate.

The enemy, on the other hand, will steal your joy and your peace, just to leave you devastated. He will crush your self-esteem just to leave you feeling empty inside. He will destroy your marriage, your health, even your reputation, just to leave you hopeless. He has no reconstruction plan. His goal is destruction of your faith in God – at all cost.

Remember Job's story?

When God points to Job as a man of faith, Satan scoffs and suggests that Job remains faithful only because his life has been blessed. If truly tested, Satan believes that any person, including Job, will stray. The Lord said to Satan, "Very well, then, everything he has is in your power, but on the man himself do not lay a finger."
(Job 1:12)

What follows is a series of tragedies, including the death of his children, that leads Job's own wife to say, "Are you still maintaining your integrity? Curse God and die!" (Job 2:9)

But Job stood his ground, clinging to God, his faith unwavering and indestructible. The devil has one goal in mind: to make you renounce your God. He steals, kills, and destroys for that very reason.

When I finally realized this truth, I felt liberated. It was the devil who stole my innocence when I was raped as a teenager. It was the devil who stole my joy when depression and anxiety made me feel dead inside. It was the devil who stole my peace when I was buried in stress. It was the devil who stole my health and nearly killed me on three different occasions. It's only by God's redemptive power that my mind and body are being restored day-by-day.

The enemy also tried to strike me down with emotional wounds, the most difficult being many years of rejection by my biological parents. My mom shunned me because I took a stand for Christ and chose not to associate with people who worshipped other gods. My dad didn't want anything to do with me either, and when we did occasionally talk, he'd say hurtful things that made me feel unwanted or dumb (despite grades that ranked 1st, 2nd, or 3rd highest in my class).

Through these situations, I believe the devil was trying to make me renounce God, just like he did with Job. Instead, God's work in me improved my self-concept and helped reconstruct these relationships. My mom became a Christian, herself, a few years later, and my dad often texts to check on me and my kids. None of us are perfect, but, thank God, we sure have come a long way.

When we go through life's challenges, it's easy to ignore God's blessings. It's in those times that we are spiritually at our weakest points and vulnerable to more of the devil's lies. We tend to become so consumed with our troubles that we forget to praise Him, and it becomes easier to neglect prayer and meditation. When we are not feeding on God's Word, nor talking to Him through prayer, it's easier for the devil to harm us. That's a scheme of the evil one. Instead of clinging to God when life is hard, the devil wants us to walk away from our ever-present source of strength, God Himself (Psalm 46:1). Don't let the devil do that to you!

How strong is your faith? Will you denounce the devil's schemes and reclaim the life that you have been so richly given in Christ? Feed yourself spiritually through prayer, reading the Scripture, and fellowship, and you'll have the tools to stand against the devil and live abundantly!

We already have this abundant life that we want.
Like I shared before, from the beginning of my Christian walk, I believed that a full life was given to me when I accepted God's word to be true. In retrospect, the reason why I did not actually feel like I was living an abundant life is pretty clear – I left the gift unopened.

After spending more time in the Scripture, I grabbed on to John 14:27: "Peace I leave with you; my peace I give you. I do not give to you as the world gives. Do not let your hearts be troubled and do not be afraid." For all those years, I simply looked at the gift, perhaps believing that a wounded person like me didn't deserve it when all I had to do was to humbly accept the gift. I had to learn to say, "Thank you, Lord, for your gift of peace. I accept it. Peace is mine right now."

Having accepted the gift, now I had to open it....to access it...to use it. When challenging situations came up, I asked myself, 'What would a peaceful person do in this moment?' I started living out the peace I knew was mine and things started to changed. I didn't feel as anxious...I was calm...I felt at peace.

Today, this feeling of peace grounds me, sustains me, and carries me through every challenge. No matter how hectic my life gets, this inner peace keeps me going. No matter what comes my way, it is well within me. That's what accepting and living an abundant life of peace does for me. It can do the same for you. You just have to accept it, open it, and use it.

A full life is not only peace. For me, it is also joy. "…Do not grieve, for the joy of the LORD is your strength." (Nehemiah 8:10). This was a game changer. When I think of all that the devil has stolen, killed, and destroyed in my life, grief is almost inevitable, but this verse tells me to find strength through joy in the Lord. And I sure did!

I started delighting in the things of God instead of my sorrows. I focused on what He has called me to do: inspire, counsel, and coach people to rise above their circumstances; and my problems appeared smaller and smaller. Don't get me wrong, they didn't go away and sometimes they become worse. After all, it's the devil's goal to stir up trouble when he sees us serving God. Today, instead of wallowing in those misfortunes, I call them out for what they are – the devil's schemes and distractions. I can find joy in serving God because I know that the battle is already won and my work is not in vain (1 Corinthians 15:58).

The more I practiced this, the easier it became and the more joyful I felt. This joy is not dependent on who is in my life and who isn't. This joy is not dependent on who accepts me or rejects me. This joy is not dependent on how healthy I am or how much money I have in my bank account. This joy is unshakeable because it's grounded on who God is and the fact that He already loves me, accepts me, and has a great purpose for my life. Do you want this joy? The world and all the people in it can't provide it. You must hang out with Jesus a bit more.

Christ paid for all our sins and shortcomings when He died on the cross. It's up to you to receive this forgiveness and live it out. Live "as if" you are forgiven, guided, protected, and cared for. How much lighter life would be if we claimed God's promises, instead of rehashing our problems? When we accept all these things and live as if we have them, life becomes more peaceful and joyful.

Psalm 16:11 says "You will make known to me the path of life; in your presence is fullness of joy; in Your right hand there are pleasures forever." These pleasures don't just happen when you get to heaven. They are forever, which means they are past, present, and future. Right now, while you are living in this fallen world, you can enjoy all that is yours in Christ. Eternal life is living forever but abundant life is experiencing joy, peace, providence, protection, and even fun right here in the land of the living. But first you have to refute the devil's schemes, receive the gift of abundant life and live it out because it's already yours!

The Secret to Beauty

BY STEPHANIE MILLER

I struggle with calling myself beautiful. When I look in the mirror, I don't see beauty. I see...well, a tired, and overwhelmed woman who is sporting braces for the second time in her life.

Once I look past the metal on my teeth, I see someone who doesn't really know what she's doing, but likes to pretend she does. Physically, I see someone who is slightly overweight, even after losing all of her baby weight and then some, but having gone through extreme dieting to get there. I see someone who still isn't happy with the way she looks. I see someone who, now carrying her second child, feels fat instead of pregnant. I look like I just had one too many tacos and maybe an extra slice of cake.

If I'm left to define beauty based on appearance, especially my own, I will miss the mark every time. Thank goodness true beauty isn't meant to be measured that way.

Genuine beauty isn't based on the way we look; it is based on the fact that God created us beautifully in His image.

Does your outside match your inside? Do you think that your body reflects the kind of person you are on the inside?

Ever since I was a little girl, I've had self-esteem issues. When you don't think you are pretty enough, smart enough or good enough, you shut yourself down and avoid situations that call for

11

you to think highly of yourself.

As an overweight child, I used food as an escape. I used it to numb my feelings, so I didn't have to internalize what was going on in my unstable and unpredictable family. Binge eating and extreme dieting were my attempts to take control of my life, and the result was measured by how I felt in a certain pair of pants or what the number on the scale said. I hated my body and the way I looked, so I would constantly punish myself for not being prettier or thinner.

When you don't feel beautiful, you don't act beautiful, because after all, you can't adopt a way of thinking until you first believe it. If you're anything like me, you have a hard time accepting compliments. When someone says I'm beautiful, I smile and say thank you, but deep down I don't really believe it. When friends comment on my smile being sweet and genuine (even through the metal wires and brackets), I dismiss their statements. Instead, I tell myself they pity me, and they are just trying to be nice. When my husband gushes over my body now and the way I look, I don't believe it because I tell myself that he is just trying to butter me up for physical intimacy later.

What would it look like, though, if when someone told us we are beautiful, instead of dismissing their compliment, we embraced it?

What if we said thank you, not as an attempt to change the conversation, but as an acknowledgement that they are building us up? We wouldn't default to pity or manipulation as a reason for their kind words, but instead see it as their way of pointing out something beautiful in us.

We can build others up by providing more than just encouragement and compliments; we can build each other up by affirming one another's godly character. If you like her confidence or her sense of humor, tell her. If you are touched by her compassionate heart, tell her that, too. We are so quick to throw out superficial compliments and deflect compliments related to our appearance, but really our character is what matters. Are we showing God's love to one another in the way that people see Christ in us? Way too many times there are things people do or words they say that really encourage or affirm us, but they never know because we never tell them. 1 Thessalonians 5:11 (NIV) tells us to: "Therefore encourage one another and build each other up, just as in fact you are doing."

That, my friends, is what beauty is. Beauty isn't looking a certain way or acting a certain way. Beauty is embracing who we are in Christ.

*"You are beautiful because God made you,
and God doesn't make mistakes. You are beautiful because
you have a purpose to fulfil as the daughter of the king."*

Honestly, we are all beautiful because we have been created by God. Everything God creates is beautiful in its unique and special way. He says in Ecclesiastes 3:11 (NIV): "He has made everything beautiful in its time. He has also set eternity in the human heart; yet no one can fathom what God has done from beginning to end."

The secret to beauty is revealed as a paradox: While outward beauty will fade (hello aging!), true beauty grows as you grow closer to God. In 2 Corinthians (4:16) we find "outwardly we are wasting away, but inwardly we are being renewed". This is good news because we are told that, "the Lord looks at the heart," (see 1 Samuel 16:7).

Plain and simple, you are beautiful because God created you in His own image. You are beautiful because you have a purpose to fulfill as the daughter of the King (see Genesis 1:27).

Recently, I was in the car with my grandmother, driving back to her house after a weekend trip. As we were almost home, the sun was setting and the way the clouds were scattered against the red, orange, and gold background, elements of mystery and beauty were added to the evening sky. While I noticed it, I didn't really think twice about it but my grandmother became overwhelmed and in awe.

"It's so beautiful!" she exclaimed.
"How could anyone say there is no God after seeing something as beautiful as that sunset?"

In all honesty, my initial reaction was, "It's just a sunset, Grandma."

But, after thinking about it, I was struck with two other thoughts:

I wish I could appreciate God's beauty in creation the way my grandmother does. God whispered back to me, "You can. You can choose to acknowledge and appreciate the beauty around you that I have created." The way my grandmother marvels at the beauty of the sunset is much like the way God marvels at us. He is pleased with us because He made us (see Genesis 1:31).

Consider the following quote from Lisa Bevere: "God uniquely created your DNA and knit your frame in secret so he could surprise the world. He authored how your heart expresses itself; He was the architect of your smile and the melody of your voice; He made all of your features with the fondest thoughts of only you in mind. He celebrated along with your parents your first smile and watched with affection your first steps."

Let that sink in for a moment. Knowing that God looks at us with such delight helps us focus not on our insecurities, but on our strengths.

My stomach, flabby and covered with stretch marks, is beautiful because it carried my daughter for 9 months. That same stomach will grow again and most likely collect more stretch marks as our new little one grows inside of me. It is beautiful. I don't have to search for what is beautiful; I only need to appreciate what God has made.

Weighing less won't make you more beautiful, nor will dying your hair a different color or putting on more makeup. What makes you beautiful isn't wearing a certain size or having perfect teeth. What makes you beautiful is that you are made in the image of God and that God was intentional and deliberate when He made you. What makes you beautiful is not a feeling — it is understanding and appreciating God's unique design and creation.

Read the following Psalm over and over again. Let this truth wash over you today, sweet friend. You are beautiful. "I praise you because I am fearfully and wonderfully made; your works are wonderful; I know that full well." Psalm 139:14 NIV

Scripture References

"For we are God's handiwork, created in Christ Jesus to do good works, which God prepared in advance for us to do." Ephesians 2:10

"Therefore, we do not lose heart. Though outwardly we are wasting away, yet inwardly we are being renewed day by day." 2 Corinthians 4:16 NIV

"The Lord does not look at the things people look at. People look at the outward appearance, but the Lord looks at the heart." 1 Samuel 16:7 NIV

"So God created mankind in his own image, in the image of God he created them; male and female he created them." Genesis 1:27 NIV

"God saw all that he had made, and it was very good." Genesis 1:31 NIV

I Am Blessed

BY PAULA MILLAR

I heard them before I saw them. The laughter and chatter coming from the neighbor's yard was a familiar sound on Saturday mornings. My childhood home was in a small neighborhood where the lawns were spacious and the children active. The obligatory peek outside confirmed that my friends were starting to gather next door. I quickly traded my pajamas for shorts and a t-shirt. I may have called for my sisters to join, but more likely I simply hollered to my parents that I was going outside to play. The heavy, wooden, front door was already open for the day, putting my target in sight. Still barefoot, I went barreling down the stairs and ran right out the door. I should say I ran right *through* the door. My 6-year-old brain forgot that a glass storm door was a firm barrier between me and the outside world. My highspirited momentum landed me out on the front porch where I stopped dead in my tracks. I stood frozen and wide-eyed with shattered glass all around me. The commotion got my mom's attention immediately. She ran out to assess the damage to me (and the front door.) Somehow, I came through with only a few small scrapes. I didn't even need a band-aid. It was remarkable. God was watching over me that day. I was blessed.

I think of this story a lot in relation to my existence. I frequently use the word "blessed" to describe my life. God has been good. I grew up in a safe, loving family. I had the privilege of a solid education. I married, raised a family of my own, and am currently enjoying my first grandchild. My health is sound and my relationships strong. I am at the end of a wonderful and long career as a school counselor. Of course, the glass panels in my world haven't always been smooth. Living in our broken world means surviving regular chips and splinters of glass. Marriage, kids, friendships, and career can be hard. As beautiful as life can be, the shards are plentiful. On my daily commute, I often thought of the issues I confronted every day at work as a giant windshield that was cracked and sectioned off into many chunks. Most of them were unattractive with jagged borders including themes of abuse, death, family dysfunction, drugs, self-destruction, chaos, trauma, and tragedy. My job was to help kids see through their imperfect, fragile, glass surfaces and find the hope and success they deserved. Although ever-present, the biggest cracks in my life were still on the periphery. I could see and hear them, and I most definitely could feel them, but the sharpest edges belonged to other people. The devastation was theirs. Even when serious issues seeped into my personal life, they were mostly with extended friends and family. I remained present, but unscathed. The scrapes existed, but there was no real blood. I was blessed.

Surrounded by other people's turmoil, I often wondered how I would respond if tragedy struck me directly. By nature, I am empathetic. I believe it was one of the greatest gifts God bestowed upon me. I am certain that part of His plan and purpose was for me to assist others in their times of need. While I could never fully understand the layers of other people's tragedies, I always strived to put myself in their place. Part of helping them was trying to relate to their plight. I gained deep admiration for those who survived serious challenges with courage and strength. I loved it when people found the blessings through the tears. I cherished those that kept their conviction in God's greater plan. Would I do the same? Would my faith waiver? What would I do when confronted by a real test? After all, while the window pane of my life was full of nicks, it was still intact. On October 20, 2018, all that changed.

I had just settled in to watch the final baseball game of the

National League Champion Series. My stomach was in knots. I take sports seriously and my Brewers finally positioned themselves to make it back to the World Series with one more win. It was going to be a big night. Obviously, I was donned in Brewer blue. My superstitious winning strategy required that, despite the smell of freshly melted cheese, I had to wait until the start of the game to eat the nachos that had just come out of the oven. It was just moments away. The sound of whistling from my cell phone meant my kids were texting as we always do for big games. My husband, Tom, wasn't participating in the texts. That was not surprising as he was with his buddies in Madison for the weekend. They were on their annual guys' trip. They had gone to the Badger football game that afternoon, and they were likely at a sports bar to watch the baseball game. I was engrossed in the pre-game warm-ups when there was a knock at the door. I was miffed at the interruption. Agitated, I yelled, "Come in!" but the visitor opted to stay outside (a test of my door-opening skills perhaps?).

My electrician hadn't yet hooked up the porch lights, so the darkening sky wouldn't allow me a preview of who was disrupting my big night. I opened the door to find a stranger. He identified himself as a deputy from the sheriff's department. What? Had he gotten lost on a dead-end road? I could help, but he'd better make it quick. By now I was sure I was missing the first pitch. He must not be a Brewer's fan. Slow and deliberate, he started to ask several questions about my husband. Then it hit me. My glass was about to fracture. My increasingly heavy heart-beat was loud enough to do some serious damage.

The deputy was gentle and kind, but I was overcome with fear and didn't return the gesture. He asked if he could come in and talk with me. I didn't want him to come in. His presence meant something bad. If I invited him in, he was going to tell me the news. Promptly, I went from not wanting to listen to wanting to know what he knew faster than he could talk. He came in, but I didn't want to sit down as he suggested. That would take too long. "Tell me now, here in my entryway." "OK, I'll sit down right here on the steps."

The rest of the exchange came in fragments, much like the texture of a glass sheet that broke into a thousand pieces. I didn't completely understand his words. I heard them only in chunks. They were sharp, uneven, and out of place. "Tom. Horrible car accident. Two cars. Roll over. CPR administered. Wisconsin Dells. Alive. Critical condition. Airlifted. University Hospital. Number for a social worker. What do you need?" What do I need? How could I know! Right now, I can't think. I can't breathe. Pacing. Frantic. I need to call my kids. I can't call my kids because I don't know enough yet.

This must be a mistake. The guys were going to be in Madison for the whole weekend. They weren't in the Dells! They've got the wrong guy. Yes. That's it. I'll call the other wives to confirm. Wait. I don't have any of their numbers. My cell phone is barely charged. How could I let that happen? I don't know what to do. More pacing. Why is this stupid baseball game still on?

Somehow, I had the presence of mind to call my sister. Within a half hour, we had friends come over to help think through what the next steps needed to be. We had to prepare for a six-hour drive toward an unknown situation. While they packed my bags, I was finally able to reach an ICU nurse. We may have talked for twenty minutes or two. After she said, "fractured vertebrae," I tuned out. I do remember asking, "Will he survive?" Her response was a measured, "We don't know for sure, but we think so." Well at least I could finally call my kids. I would be taking a sledge hammer to their panes of glass.

An hour after the knock on my door, my sister and I left for Madison. We were five miles down the road when she pulled into the parking lot of our favorite diner. "We are going to pray," she said. It felt odd. We had a long night ahead of us and we had never in our lives just stopped to pray. Yes…praying was the right thing to do. I don't remember the words she used. I remember the tears and the sense of calm this brought. I remember knowing that, no matter the outcome of this terrible day, I would be OK.

On the road to Madison, I made many calls to family and friends, including family members of the other men in the accident. I was devastated to hear that Tom's friend, Scot, died at the scene. The other three were all airlifted to the University Hospital. I found out that Tom had a spinal fracture, ten broken ribs, a severely dislocated knee, a torn ureter, and a foot that was only hanging on by some skin.

We got to the hospital at 2 a.m. Tom had just come out of surgery for his foot. His leg was in a contraption that looked like a large erector set. He had a breathing tube in. He was wearing a neck brace to keep his spine stable. He was hooked up to machines and somewhat responsive. He was alive. We are blessed.

The days, weeks, and now months that followed have been almost indescribable. Our friend Dave succumbed to his injuries after 11 days. As for the survivors, their healing may never be complete. For my husband, the fracture in his vertebrae ended up not being the primary concern. His severed foot was saved but then became severely infected. We continue with the uncertainty of whether he will walk again, and if so, to what extent.

We also experienced beautiful gestures. We connected with the stranger who was the first person to approach the accident scene. She had held my husband's hand and talked with the guys while they awaited the ambulance. We also learned about some passers-by on the highway who stopped on the road to form a prayer circle. Additionally, our extended circle of family and friends created prayer groups across the country.

Tom was in the hospital and far from our home for over two months. My empathetic nature came with a price: as Tom's days go so do mine. He was able to get his mood up when he had visitors, but he had nothing left in him when they were gone. I didn't blame him. He needed to get through his days, tethered to a bed, as best as he could. Therefore, I spent a lot of time sitting alone at the hospital. In that healing environment, I focused a lot on my blessings. I reflected on my past and my future. I remembered the many people who have survived tragedy and their attitudes and approach.

I thought a lot about life and God and faith and prayer. I sat in the hospital lounge, reciting the prayers I learned in my Catholic upbringing. I thought about the meaning of those prayers. I came up empty. My blessings seem to have run out.

Despite many wonderful visitors, phone calls, cards, and messages, my hospital time was lonely. I tried to rely on my personal strength and belief system, but my recent thoughts of blessings and prayer continued to nag at me. If I had always felt blessed by my life circumstances, what did that mean about my current reality? Was I still blessed or had I lost favor with God? If I didn't really know how to pray outside of my neat and orderly box, was it still prayer? If I didn't really understand these things, what has my supposed walk with God really been about? Maybe I have gotten a lot of things wrong.

Over the next several months, I used the gift of time that God had bestowed upon me. While my Catholic upbringing had laid the foundation for my faith, I simply had to go deeper. I needed to understand God's will. I began to read, research, and discuss the biblical approach to being Christian. In turn, I opened a dialogue with God. I thought a lot about all the prayer warriors on our behalf. I could literally feel the energy from them. I could feel the presence of greatness. When I paused to recognize it, I could feel Jesus wrapping His arms around my tired soul and telling me I was not alone. He wanted me to feel Him, but even more than that, he wanted me to trust Him.

God certainly got my attention. Was that a reason for the accident? That is not for me to know. I only know that I the accident renewed my passion for connecting with God. This has been a blessing. I am learning new ways to pray.

Knowing and loving God is an honor. What I used to consider His blessings were simply earthly gifts. Sometimes those gifts blinded me. While I always appreciated them and thanked God for them, I became complacent. It is easy to trust God when our earthly gifts feel sufficient. However, we were never promised comfort. In fact, we were promised suffering and hardship. This is when our faith is tested. The real gifts come when we follow Christ as our pathway to God and to eternal life. I was never tasked to be strong. I was tasked to ask Christ to be my strength, my patience, my comfort, my joy. Being blessed is not about being happy. Circumstances are not what make us blessed. Our hearts and our unconditional love for God are our greatest blessings. I am blessed.

Change is Coming

BY JOY TRACHSEL

"Isn't it funny how day by day nothing changes, but when you look back, everything is different..." -C.S. Lewis

I will never forget the day my husband and I dropped off our youngest child at college. Once the last box was unpacked and the futon properly assembled, we said our goodbyes and made the drive home. For the first time in almost 30 years, we were returning to a home without children.

Adjusting to an "empty nest" was challenging at first. A lot of changes came at once. The laundry pile was smaller, the pizza order was smaller, and the house was a lot quieter. Change came without my permission or approval.

Of course, I always knew that day was coming. God willing, every baby becomes a toddler and the goodbyes as they go off to daycare, pre-school, grade school and junior and senior high, are made less traumatic for us parents by knowing they'll be coming home at the end of the day. We prepare them for independence and hope they'll carry some of mom and dad's wisdom with them into adulthood. It's a natural and healthy progression, but not one without a few tears and long nights of looking at baby albums.

This kind of expected change is tough enough, but what about the kind that blindsides you? The shocking shake up you didn't plan or make a to-do list for. The tragic transformation that you wish was only a dream and would go back to normal when you opened your eyes. Let me give you a little dose of reality – That only happens in the movies.

We all face them. We all do our best to get through the disruptions with our faith intact. For me, they come all too often. A broken relationship, the unexpected passing of a loved one, and, most recently, a deep bout of depression – All of these changes came into my life uninvited. As a Christian, I have listened to many sermons on God's plan and how He uses tough times to strengthen us. Oh, how much easier it would be change came without hurt, suffering, and disruption of what we feel is a pretty good life." I will never forget when my "pretty good life" became unrecognizable.

One of the darkest times of my life began on November 3, 2016, and lasted for several months. The experience is still raw, but on that day, I began suffering what I now know to be a mental breakdown. Depression isn't something that is new to me. For the last 15 years, I have struggled with small bouts of depression and anxiety. It never had a huge impact on my day-to-day living and I had learned to manage the occasional "blues." This time it was different. I never found myself wanting to harm myself, but I did pray that God would take me home and allow happiness to be present, even if it meant me leaving earth. As I look back on this time, it reminds me to be grateful that only God knows what lies ahead of us. If I had known how long I was going to be struggling, I am not sure I would have been able to persevere. Praise God that He is in control and not us.

"I knew what I had to do. I had to "lay it down,
The God that presented himself to me was not going to be ignored.
He stepped in to save me from myself."

Six months before, my world began to spin out of control.

I noticed an unsettling restlessness within me. Family and friends expressed concern. I even heard a gentle whisper from God telling me I was treading on dangerous ground spiritually. I tuned everybody out, insisting that the way I was living my life was best. There was absolutely no reason I thought that I needed to change anything. I finally had everything that I wanted - a big office, a fancy title and some money. I was able to impact the lives of others and it all came under the name of "ministry."

It all came to a tipping point on that November day when happiness seemed to disappear and extreme depression settled in. I went to bed at noon and didn't move for the next 30 hours. Those hours looked like a desperate woman, numb and lifeless. Cries to God seemed to be unheard. Eventually, I was able to leave my bed for short periods of time, but for several more weeks, I'd return to that cocoon, overcome by mental anguish and a belief that any kind of happiness was non-existent.

Looking back, I know this didn't happen out of the blue or without reason. It was a physical, emotional and spiritual response to attaching myself to a false idol. To me, an idol is anything that comes ahead of God. It isn't always material. It's some 'thing' or some feeling that distracts my heart and mind from a loving Father: A car or a home; Ambition or a relationship; Even potentially selfish service to others. The idol that kept me away from my true God was a combination of all these things. I had been living my life on my own terms and filling God-shaped voids with ambition, influence, and a career. I realized that some of what kept me in that depression was a reliance on things that did not glorify God. My attention was given to false truths that were from the world and not from my faith.

I knew what I had to do. I had to "lay it down." It was time to stop pretending that I had it all figured out and that I could maintain a healthy spiritual life while making bad choices. Bad choices such as seeking affirmation from a career and looking for the attention and approval of others. I vividly remember the night that I decided to lay it down. There was finally an inner peace and emptiness at the same time. I went to bed that night emotionally exhausted and scared. The question spinning through my mind was "how do I rebuild?"

I would love to be able to write that an instant transformation came over me and I awoke to a new life.

What happened was the opposite.

The more I thought about re-dedicating my full self to God, the more I rationalized why that wasn't really necessary. With this newfound self-knowledge, I was certain that I could make some minor changes and keep self-seeking ambition in my life. For a while, things seemed right and normal again. My work and ministry filled spiritual voids. A sense of purpose returned.

The God that presented himself to me was not going to be ignored though. He stepped in to save me from myself once again. The following weeks were challenging. I prayed for immediate answers and was hurt by what I believed was God's silence. I was frustrated, confused, and uncomfortable. Unwilling to abide by God's will and accept the change He wanted for me, I gave myself once again to the false idol.

How sad. How sad that I thought I knew better than my Creator. How sad that I thought I knew better than the Divine.

It reminds me of a time when I encountered a sweet young woman struggling with drugs. I was hoping she would allow me to drive her to rehab but the offer was refused. She expressed an incredible desire to get clean but simply couldn't muster the willingness to take the first step. Incredibly, she told me she was hoping to get arrested so she would be forced (by external circumstances) to get the drugs out of her system and maybe, just maybe, be able to make a clear-headed decision about her future. When she shared that with me, I suddenly understood what she meant. Just like my friend, I didn't have the strength to do what I needed to do by myself so God, again not willing to be ignored, essentially forced the change...He removed the idol from my life.

What followed was a dark time of healing, counseling, and many visits to various doctors. It wasn't a quick process, but I came through it CHANGED!

Hebrews 13:8 teaches us that Jesus never changes. He is the same yesterday, today, and tomorrow. Praise God that He remains unchanged while initiating huge change in us. It is only through Him that we can change in a way that makes us look more like Jesus.

Praise God that He uses our tears, our struggles, and even our darkest moments to make us better.

The process can be painful. As I look back on the change God created in my life, I am reminded of 1 Corinthians 6:11 "you were washed, you were sanctified and you were justified in the name of the Lord Jesus Christ and by the Spirit of the God." When the devil was removed from me, the cleansing and washing began. True change took root.

How do you respond to change?

Does it propel you forward toward fulfillment? Does it push you backward into familiar patterns that leave you listless?

My prayer is that whenever change comes your way, you look upward toward the heavens. Change is hard but one thing remains... Jesus.

Simply Chosen
BY TRACY LOKEN WEBER

"For many are invited, but few are chosen."
Matthew 22:14

Everywhere we go, we want to be accepted, to belong, for us to be chosen. But I wonder what it would be like, really feel like, if we already knew with all our heart that we are already chosen by Christ.

No matter how you look at it, all at some point in our lives we have all wanted to be chosen. Do you remember being in gym class and the coach randomly selects two team captains? Next, as the captains choose their teammates one-by-one, you desperately hope not to be the last one picked. No one ever wants to be left out, the last one picked, or forgotten.

Now flash forward to your first job. Filling out an application, submitting your resume, putting on a new outfit to make the best first impression possible. The interview comes and goes. You send a nice thank you as a follow-up and wait...and wait. You hope and pray that they will choose you for the position - choose you to be on their team.

Every single day we are faced with so many choices. Would you believe that researchers say we make over 35,000 decisions a day? 35,000 choices. Before we even leave the house, we choose whether to pray, what cereal to eat, and 'What should I wear today? Pants, capris, shorts? Behind the wheel, there are a half-dozen gas stations from which we choose where to fill up our tank, and at every intersection, we choose whether it's best to go right, left, or straight and if you happen to go to the grocery store that day? My goodness! I'd bet the number of choices we make is tripled. How many cheeses are the right number of cheeses on a frozen pizza? Do I want apples to bake with, or apples to eat? Or, is it going to be that kind of day where every choice is going to be an indulgence? Candy, chips, dips, and more? A small, medium or large coffee or soda? Skim milk, 2% or almond milk? The choices are endless. And yet what an amazing world we live in to have the freedom and luxury to make these decisions.

Of course, many of our daily decisions affect more than our bank balance. We are confronted in 'Aha! moments' by choices that may be life-changing. These moments, often unforeseen, can define our next steps, actions, and choices for years to come. From falling in love, moving to a new city, changing careers, finding a new church family, to managing our health. I will never forget the moment my doctor said to me, "You have cancer." In one brief moment, my life changed.

Being recently engaged, so many thoughts came to mind. Thoughts of 'will the man of my dreams still marry me?' to 'I will never be able to experience childbirth, to bond with a precious child that my husband and I created.' Those decisions were not in my hands, but the choice to embrace five years of healing, to keep moving forward and to seek out health was all mine. No one else could do it for me. My actions, my behaviors, and my healing were all choices that I had to make.

Even though I was not able to physically have children, my husband and I chose to become foster parents. We chose to seek out a group of siblings at risk of being separated in the foster care system. We chose to create a forever family, we chose love. Little did we know how much these little hearts would change us, how many aha! moments we would have, and how our lives would forever change.

Recently, on a sunny spring morning, it was a great fresh start to the day and a family first – each of our three amazing adopted children kissed me goodbye before they left for school. They attend three different schools, with three different bus pick up times, three hours apart. My ten-year-old son kissed me on the cheek and said that I was the best mom ever. Our nine-year-old daughter hugged and kissed me goodbye, having snuck a special note in my computer with the most encouraging and heartfelt words: Dear Mommy, I hope you have a great day working on your paper. You are the world's best and smartest mommy ever. I love you to the moon and back and around the sun and back around all the planets!!! This was followed by a hug and kiss from our seven-year-old daughter telling me that I am the best mommy she's ever had because I'm the one that never hurts her, makes her feel safe, and throws dance parties.

And just like that, I felt like a huge Mack truck just hit me. The grace of God's love was unfolding before my eyes. Never-ending love and grace coming full-circle. God's love stirring in their little hearts is put into motion for His will. His purpose was for our married life to be something greater. Greater than 'Poor me, my illness took away the chance to have biological children', but rather, 'Yay us, we get to provide a safe, stable, and loving home for three siblings who'd been separated for two years.' My illness and our choices allowed this sibling group to be baptized in faith and live together. To run free and have a care-free youth, swinging on the playset in our backyard. To go to summer camp, sit by a campfire, and just be a child without grownup concerns. These precious children of God were chosen just for us.

You see, sometimes when you are not looking, you may just be called to action.

When you listen, truly listen, and take a leap of faith --- your choices can make a lasting impact.

When was the last time that you stopped to look at the beauty all around you? The beautiful shades of white clouds high up in the sky moving ever so slowly. The prairie grasses swaying in the field with an old majestic oak tree standing so very tall. The tiniest of individual little snowflakes, each unique and gracefully falling from the sky. How about observing the change of seasons, the leaves altering colors and beautiful tulips are beginning to bloom. As you take in all of these beautiful creations of God, remember when you look in the mirror, you too are His creation. Made to be just you, beautiful, strong, smart, resilient, and here on this earth to make a lasting impact. God chose you.

Dear Beautiful You
This is your life, your day, your moment
(your very own life)
Get to know your soul, your inner self, your inner voice
Dance your dance, bust a move
Sing your song, loud and proud
Take charge of your story and be intentional
every second of every day
Love your day, every second, minute, hour
Let your heavy burdens go, bless and release
Pray your prayers, pray for others and pray like a warrior
Pour your heart out to God,
he already knows what your heart has on it
Embrace your blessings, every single one of them
Kiss your beloveds, daily
Give thanks in all you do, all you have, all the blessings
Forgive your mistakes, we all have them
Forgive your enemies, you know who they are
Take time to heal your pain, breathe, heal,
give yourself time Rest your body, your mind,
be one with nature, take time for you
Share your God given gifts and talents,
don't be shy --- shine bright
Practice your passions and share with others

Find your bliss and do something you enjoy every day
Live Your Life; Love Your Life Because God has Chosen You
God has Chosen You.

Beautiful you, just think about it. In this moment in time, you are already chosen. Now, what are you choosing? Are you choosing to make decisions that are God pleasing? Saying yes to following God's word and being open to trusting His timing. Remembering with every choice you make, I am guided by God's will, His plan for me.

So, do you need a reboot? Do you feel like you are missing something in your life right now?

Pause for a few minutes. Take time to do some soul-searching and personal reflection. Pause and consider: What am I really wanting to do that I just keep putting off?

Is it making amends with a friend or family member? Maybe a calling to slow down and be present for your family? To turn off that cell phone and be with your family? To dive deeply into His word? To lead a home bible study? To pray more with your children? To appreciate nature? Remember those 35,000 daily decisions? That amounts to more than 2,320,000 over a lifetime. With every decision, there will be some form of cause and effect. The choices are yours, and yours alone, to make. Think about it – Making one slight adjustment to your daily routine can have a lasting impact on your overall perspective on life, attitudes, and relationship with God and others.

So, what will you choose? I encourage you to set aside some time the next few days or hours to create ten-to-twenty "I am" or "I will" statements. Statements that you can reflect on every single day. Say these statements out loud. Say them with conviction, believing each with your whole heart. All the while knowing that you are a child of God. You have been chosen to make an everlasting impact for good. It is my hope that my "I am" statements will inspire the creation of your own.

I Am CHOSEN
I am choosing to be a Child of God.
I am Hopeful for the future.
I am Open to giving and receiving love.
I am a vessel Shining bright like a beacon of God's love
to all those I come in contact with.
I am keeping my Eyes on Jesus, being in His word and
showing His grace to others.
I am living my best life Now,
being present and believing in myself.

I Will
I will be open to receive and give love.
I will embrace each day with a new hope of faith, love and joy.
I will make the most of the time God has given me.
I will take care of myself allowing time for hydration,
rest and personal care.
I will be mindful of my choices and stay true to who I am.
I will be an influence of change helping those who need to be lifted
up and encouraged.

What you decide to do every day matters. What will your choices be? What will you choose to do? The future is yours. It's in your hands. God is waiting for you. So boldly go out into the world, be a beacon of light to others and spread the grace of being chosen in Christ with every single person you come into contact with. For it is through Him, His grace that you are forgiven and set free, you, dear child of God --- are chosen.

Finally, all of you, be like-minded, be sympathetic,
love one another, be compassionate and humble.
1 Peter 3:8

In Christ

BY TRACY LOKEN WEBER

"Therefore, as God's chosen people, holy and dearly loved, clothe yourselves with compassion, kindness, humility, gentleness and patience." Colossians 3:12

Poets, musicians, and even us "regular" people endlessly pose and ponder questions of "Why?"

Why am I in this difficult place?

Why does God keep giving me so much to handle?

Why am I the chosen one?

Throughout my life, like any one of us, I've faced some extremely difficult situations. Professionally, I even placed myself in tough spots; working with teachers and administrators to minimize disparities in the education system, providing insight and guidance to save financially-stricken organizations on the brink of collapse. Even with a diverse career, all of these experiences left me wanting more.

An inner voice summoned me to make a significant difference in the life of a child. Specifically, a calling to provide a safe and loving home for siblings who had been separated by the foster care system.

In the midst of a teaching career, I won the lottery! An

amazing man entered my life. Having met on eHarmony, my guy happened to live 12 hours away. Now don't get me wrong, that can have its advantages. But soon enough, despite the distance, we talked about a future as husband and wife.

One year into our relationship, one of those extremely difficult situations nearly nixed any chance at a future together (or alone for that matter). On an ominous day in May, I was diagnosed with uterine cancer. An immediate hysterectomy was the doctor's recommendation.

I was in shock as I walked out of the examination room.

The nursing staff lined the hallway for moral support. It was surreal. Did the doctor really say what I think she said?

Cancer?
Hysterectomy?

Looking into the nurses' faces, I knew I heard the doctor correctly and my life would be forever changed.

As I left the doctor's office, a new reality was sinking in. I had cancer and I needed to do something about it right away. Unfortunately, that 'something' would rule out any chance of becoming pregnant. A flood of emotions washed over me. I broke down crying, sobbing actually, as I walked out of the building.

---

boldly go out into the world,
be a beacon of light to others and
spread the grace of being chosen in Christ...

That summer, I had two surgeries to remove the fast-growing, football-sized tumor with tentacles wrapping themselves around nearby organs. My life was saved. The operations were successful and I spent 12 long weeks recovering, during which time, the love of my life proposed. I would begin a year of physical and emotional healing while also planning the wedding of our dreams. During this time, I leaned on God's Word. I leaned on Him while reminding myself that the good Lord doesn't give us anything we can't handle even as I struggled to walk, bathe, and meet basic personal needs following the cancer surgery.

For the next few years, I couldn't hold a baby. I couldn't talk about having a baby. I was an emotional mess. I cried. I cried a lot. I was mourning the loss of a life I had so wanted to give to myself, give to my soon-to-be husband, give to a child. Through it all, my wonderful fiancé and amazing friends, family, colleagues and church community came to my side. They helped me heal - physically, emotionally and spiritually.

"For the God who calls you is faithful, and He can be trusted to make it so." – 1 Thessalonians 5:24

Our wedding day finally arrived – it was perfect! We soon moved to another state, and our lives continued. New friends who didn't know my story started asking the question every newlywed couple hears: "When are you going to get pregnant?!" I would get teary eyed and simply respond, "Maybe someday."

After being married for five years, we began praying for God's hand to guide our hearts to add children to our lives. Our marriage was ready to grow and welcome children in our lives. We were ready to withstand the highs and lows of finding our forever family. Either we were going to keep our normal day-to-day life or take a leap of faith and grab life with both hands and push on. The day eventually came when we were called to action.

We learned more about family services in our area and

began the demanding process of becoming foster parents: Local, state, and national background checks; multiple home inspections; classes to become licensed; employment verifications; and a review of financial records. Every single part of our lives was laid out for social services to inspect. I firmly believe that in order to grow, we had to push out of our normal, comfort zone and into the unknown. With God by our side, we took that leap of faith and trusted His hand to guide us.

Our path began by serving as a respite care home for foster families. In this role, two teenage girls were scheduled to stay with us for a weekend. Naturally, the girls were unsure of us. However, we tried to make them comfortable by laying out our plans for the next couple of days. It being autumn, we carved some pumpkins and made homemade sugar cookies, warm apple cider, and even an apple pie with fresh fruit from the local orchard. The weekend was great. We all had fun and then the girls headed back to their longer-term foster home.

The following Monday, we discovered that their foster parents thought it would be best to separate the girls. That was our cue to take action.

After contacting the county government, we were able to bring the sisters back together, providing a stable and loving home over the course of their school year. They arrived with holes in their shoes and clothes and no personal items. As a treat, we went on a little shopping spree. The girls were shocked that someone they just met cared enough to take them shopping. In reality, these two children of God only wanted to have food to eat, to fit in, and to be reunited with their mother. Grace, love and compassion for both of these girls was given without a second thought. We did so gladly, because we were able to do so.

School concerts, conferences, bake sales and field trips. Not to mention lunches, loads of laundry, nightly homework and church on Sunday. The girls often asked us if we were "real" because their other home was full of chaos and lacked any parental involvement. We prayed with them, we exposed them to the love of Christ and how through Christ all things are possible. Slowly they began to feel safe, loved and cared for. The walls they had put up to protect their hearts, slowly came down. Laughter filled the home and healing was taking place.

"Finally, all of you, be like-minded, be sympathetic, love one another, be compassionate and humble." 1 Peter 3:8

Nine months came and went. It was time for the girls to return to their mother. As we waited at the courthouse, the girls were excited to go home. When the judge ruled that they would be returned to their mother, the girls looked at me and I smiled back at them. You could see that a part of them was happy, yet a part of them was sad. As we left the courtroom, the oldest hugged my husband and me very hard, thanking us for all that we did for them, for bringing her sister back, and for all the love we'd shown them. When she came to us, the oldest was a depressed, failing, and suicidal student – after her placement with us ended, we learned she eventually graduated high school with honors, got a job, lived independently, and moved on to college in pursuit of an electrical engineering degree!

We took deep breaths as we said goodbye to those girls whom we had come to know as our foster daughters. Once they had gone, a sense of loss set in. We needed time: Time to regroup, refocus, and recharge. We learned so much about the foster care system thanks to these two girls. Unfortunately, it opened our eyes to how children can be mistreated and the lack of support for kids with special needs. We had a crash-course on mental health issues, how to obtain services, counseling, appointments, working within the school systems, and navigating social services. This was our first time, seeing with our own eyes, the dire need for good, quality foster parents that would truly provide for a child as their own.

Over the next two years, we continued to pray. We prepared to accept a placement of children on eight different occasions, but for one reason or another, it didn't happen. For example, sometimes another relative stepped up and was able to take them, or the children were being relocated out of state. We remained steadfast in the notion that sometime when the moment was right, the Lord would entrust us with the children meant for us.

Finally, in June 2015, the day came. We received a call telling us about a group of three siblings, two girls and a boy, who had been separated for over two years. We needed to let social services know right away if we can meet the little boy who was 6 years old the next day and allow him to move in within a week. The girls would follow shortly after. Quickly, we sprung into action not knowing much about the children except that they were 3, 5 and 6 years old.

Clothing, toys, bikes, and basically anything a child would love to have soon filled our home thanks to friends. Our church family showed incredible support, lovingly providing essentials to help welcome the children.

With great anticipation, excitement, and nervous energy my husband and I drove to pick up our son-to-be. Pulling up to the house, we noticed people bringing a small box and brown paper bag to the curb and then a little boy sitting on the front steps, not looking well at all. Turns out he had just returned home from the hospital where he was diagnosed with scarlet fever. The current foster parents didn't want him back in the house. And that small box and bag? Well, those were all of his belongings. Already distancing themselves from the boy, the couple waved from afar and turned to wish us a cautious, "Good luck." That was the last time we heard or saw them.

This little boy was sick – really sick. A motherly instinct kicked-in right away to care for this child. He needed pajamas,

43

clothes, shoes, a toothbrush, hairbrush, and love.

As he recovered from scarlet fever, two months of occasional home visits with his two sisters began. Three days before school began, the girls came to stay for good. When the children were reunited, the love they showed one-another could melt the iciest heart. They were inseparable. Wherever they sat, the girls surrounded their brother – On the sofa, at the kitchen table, in the pool, or walking hand-in-hand – they were together again.

God's grace embraced our new family. Patience, love, compassion, and understanding were showered on us by the church, school, and family. We needed all of that (and more). The children had been reunited for a whole three days and we had no routine, no schedule, and every morning was mass chaos. Let me tell you, only prayer got us through.

Over time, we began to understand the special needs of each child and slowly started the adoption process. Almost two years after the initial placement with our family, the court confirmed what we already knew – We were a family.

"He settles the barren woman in her home as the happy mother of children. Praise the Lord". Psalm 113:9

Two years ago, I stepped away from a career that I absolutely loved. The ability to take a step back from work to focus on our family and my PhD studies really rocked my world. Talk about taking one huge leap of faith. This hasn't been easy. In fact, being home, overseeing over twelve hours of therapy a week and ongoing special needs for our kiddos is exhausting and a thankless job. Deep down, it has been a lonely path to be on. It's hard for folks to understand the complexities of day-to-day life with children who suffer from serious trauma, ADHD, anxiety and PTSD. Every single day is hard. Really hard.

It seems that most conversations begin with "How are you?" Have you had to say that everything is "fine" just to save time and keep on moving forward? Have you felt like you're on this path alone? Trust me, you're not alone. For Christ is right there at your side, every single step of the day. No matter your hardship, He is right by your side. Every tantrum, every explosion, every manic behavioral outburst. Christ is with you. It is during this time that I stop, take a deep breath and feel His presence. I lean on Him for strength to power through each difficult moment. That's all it is, one moment that is testing our child and our faith at the same time. Together, we face our daily challenges straight on and slowly allow the healing to take place.

I believe that all of these life challenges were preparing me for the long journey of becoming a mother and children's advocate. A greater calling to provide a safe, stable, and loving home for three siblings who were separated for over two years. A chance for them to be reunited... to be siblings... to be family... part of a forever family --- together, forever.

So, questions remain. Why did God have all this happen to me? Why did I overcome cancer? Why did my husband and I find our perfect family?

Why? Maybe just "To be right here."

Right here today – Sharing my testimonial with you, being "mama" to three amazing children, and showing unwavering grace to those in need. For we truly never know the personal struggles we may encounter at any given moment in time.

God has a purpose for our struggles. Lean on Him. Trust in Him. Never give up. You are stronger than you realize and with the power of Christ working in you, you can overcome any adversity life throws your way.

Heavenly Father,

Please lay your hands on my life, guide me, let me fully trust in you and your plan. Let me rise to action when called and do what is right to help those in need. Open our hearts and minds to be present daily in Christ. To take time from the hustle and bustle to study His word. To serve not only at church but also within our community so your light can shine brightly through our thoughts, words and actions. Let us all take the Word of Christ and enter the mission field of life with grace, compassion, love, and joy. Amen.

Courage

BY CASSIE MICKLE

"Then Esther sent this reply to Mordecai: 16
Go, gather together all the Jews who are in Susa, and fast for me. Do not
eat or drink for three days, night or day. I and my attendants will fast as you
do. When this is done, I will go to the king, even though it is against the
law. And if I perish, I perish." (Esther 4:15-16, NIV)

I've never thought of myself as particularly courageous. More like strong or stubborn, maybe. Initially, I wanted to write on the word "changed", but I knew my friend Joy would do a great job with it. After praying on "courage", I knew that God chose this word for me!

Today, when I think of courage, I think of the great women in the Bible. Ruth, for example, was a woman of great courage. She was a Moabite who married an Israeli man, the son of Naomi and Elimelech. After her husband's death, Ruth chose to leave her country and accompany her mother-in-law back to Judea, for Naomi was severely depressed having also lost her own husband and second son. In Ruth's time of loss, it would have been the natural choice for her to stay in Moab with her own people (as her sister-in-law, Oprah, did). However, Ruth showed great courage in deciding to leave her homeland and care for Naomi. The Bible does not mention whether Ruth adopted the Jewish faith or not. As a Moabite woman, she would have been a follower of the god Chemosh. Her courage to put her trust in a God that she did not know much about is awe inspiring. As the story goes, she marries a relative of her husband per Jewish tradition, and she becomes an ancestor of Jesus.

Esther grew into her beauty as an orphaned member of a lowly Jewish exile community in Persia. Only her cousin, Mordecai, knew she was a Jew when King Ahasuerus chose her to be his wife. Haman, a high court official to the king, hated Mordecai and plotted to have all the Jews killed. To save the Jewish people, Queen Esther had to summon the courage to talk to her husband. Speaking to the king without permission would risk her life. She told Mordecai "If I perish, I perish." At a banquet, Esther boldly asks the king to save her life, and the lives of all her people. When asked who threatened her life, the wicked Haman was identified. Ultimately, the furious king called for Haman to be hanged on the very gallows built for Mordecai and all the Jews. Queen Esther's courage saved the Jews from genocide.

Mary, the mother of Jesus, is probably the Bible's most famous story of a woman's courage. God favored Mary and knew her faith and loyalty made her the perfect person to bear the Son of God. When the angel Gabriel approached Mary, she was told not to be afraid. Mary was thought to be 14 at the time. I don't know about you, but I'd be frightened at any age.

But Mary drew on her courage and told the angel, "Let it be as you have said," in spite of the near certainty that her fiancé Joseph would break off their engagement should she become pregnant. Pregnancy outside of marriage may not be a shameful condition today, but it goes without saying that Mary (and Joseph) would be shunned by society and struggle to survive. She knew her family and friends would abandon her.

Each of these women faced death - whether physically or socially. Each of these women obeyed God and followed His direction. Each of these women lived courageously.

I also think of the courageous Christian women in the world today who do not live in a free country. Women who live in predominantly Muslim countries like Pakistan or Sudan are not free to worship Christ. Casual conversation can land them on death row or disowned by their family. Being shunned by one's family may be sad here in the United States, but in other countries, women depend on their husbands and families to support them because opportunities for employment are few and far between.

Pain is a constant reminder that you are not whole...
find the courage within you to give
your life over to Christ in all things.

How could I think of myself as courageous when I do not face life and death choices every day? I started with a dictionary definition. One definition of courage I found is "strength in the face of pain or grief."

By that definition, every one of us has demonstrated courage at one time or another. My experiences in this way are in no way more important than my neighbor's, but I would like to share a few stories as a source of strength.

When I was two years old, I fell down a flight of stairs. I did not break any bones, but I developed lumps on my wrists and fingers. I often cried out in pain, but my parents had no idea what was wrong. Doctors dismissed it as growing pains. Then, when I was 11, after hurting my shoulder playing rough with my brother, my parents took me to the Emergency Room for an x-ray. Again, no broken bones, but the radiologist gave my parents some shocking news. My joints showed a great deal of wear and tear, and soon after, doctors diagnosed me with rheumatoid arthritis (RA).

I grew up in a home dedicated to the Lord. We went to church at least three times a week. My parents loved Jesus, and I've never known a life without Him. I knew He loved me and died for my sins. In my teenage years, I rebelled of course. I thought I knew everything and wanted to follow the ways of the world. After high school, I got married and started having children. I wanted them to know Jesus the way I did as a child so we went to church regularly and my relationship with God was renewed.

Unfortunately, my marriage eventually split apart and by my late twenties and early thirties, I started having more RA flare-ups. Doctors prescribed tons of medication, but I began to blame God for allowing me to have all this pain. I went back to my old rebellious ways.

In 2004, my son was nine when he was diagnosed with type I diabetes. It added fuel to the fire of my anger. Then in 2010, my daughter, who was 16, was diagnosed with type I diabetes, as well. My resentment toward God boiled over. I was severely depressed and often thought of suicide. I couldn't keep a relationship for longer than a few months. I was addicted to a false sense of love, which sometimes expressed itself in unfulfilling ways. Thoughts of suicide turned into plans for suicide toward the end of 2010, when, through the grace of God, I received a postcard in the mail inviting me to a new church. It was in a movie theater, and I thought to myself, 'What kind of church meets in a movie theater?!' I was curious and had to check it out.

I was blown away! I had never been to a church that was so casual. I grew up in a very rigid and legalistic churches that squashed any modicum of creativity or leanings towards "worldliness." I met some great people at that movie theater church who remain friends to this day.

I leaned on that newfound support in 2011 when a family member told me she had been raped by a man in our lives over a four-year period starting when she was 12 years-old. Grief overwhelmed me. How had I been blind to the red flags in that relationship? Blame was squarely on my shoulders, I believed, for bringing that man into our house. Even though he was caught and prosecuted for his crime, I still have nightmares about the situation and his victim struggles to overcome the evil acts committed against her.

Why has all this pain and grief come to me and my family?

That question is unanswerable by human beings. In the end, all I know is that I trust that God has a plan for all of our lives. I know He loves me deeply and will sustain us during good times and bad.

My list of ailments grows longer every month and I have been speaking to women about trusting God during health crises. It takes a great deal of courage to trust God when physical pain steals my energy, robs the joy from life, and threatens my family's finances. There are days when I'm very irritable. There are days when I think the pain will never end. I want to exercise or do things around the house, but I've got no energy. I spend thousands of dollars each year beyond my insurance premiums to pay for medications, doctor's visits, and tests. And I can't even count the amount of lost wages. Missing work makes me feel like I am not doing my job, and people are judging me. My disability is not visible, and I usually do not talk about it unless I have to.

Many people who have no health problems have trouble summoning the courage to trust God with their lives. Those of us who struggle with pain and depression find it even more difficult to cope. Pain is a constant reminder that you are not whole, you are not normal, or you are not blessed with health.

I know that God has a plan for my life. I may not even get to see it play out, but I have courage enough to place my trust in Him.

I implore each of you to find the courage within you to give your life over to Christ in all things. If you pray for a need and God says "no" or "not now", show courage and allow Him to reveal the great works in His time. Stop pounding on that closed door and wait for Him to open another.

As it says in Romans 8:28: "And we know that in all things God works for the good of those who love Him, who have been called according to his purpose."

If you see someone struggling with pain or grief, hug them, and tell them that you are praying for them and you know it takes a lot of courage to smile when you are crying inside.

I am Enough

BY JENN BAXTER

For as far back as I can remember, I felt like I wasn't enough.

Now, this wasn't always a conscious feeling – I didn't sit around all day bemoaning my existence.

But, the underlying belief about myself – the feelings that were down deep in my soul – told me that my true self wasn't enough. This distorted belief drove all of my thoughts and actions. It directed the paths I followed, the choices I made, and especially the words I spoke to myself.

And the result was an intense case of perfectionism.

Again, it wasn't necessarily something that I even consciously thought about though. Growing up, I just knew that I got straight A's in school and I liked it that way. I never said bad words. I never went out partying and drinking with my friends.

It's just how it was. I was the "good girl."

And I liked the response it brought from the world around me. Teachers enjoyed me. Strangers smiled at me. My parents didn't have to worry about me.

I guess that was how I got validation. Except that, ironically, it never felt like enough.

Over the years, I found myself beginning to "morph" into other versions of myself, depending on who was around.

When I liked a guy, I would find out all the things he liked and the suddenly become immersed in them too. If he liked punk music, that's all I would listen to. If he was a big football fan, I suddenly started paying attention to the games.

It wasn't quite as bad with my friends. I was pretty authentic with them most of the time. But I did have another underlying belief that would often affect both my crushes and my friendships.

Deep down, I believed that if someone knew me long enough... if they stuck around long enough to really know me... they'd stop liking me and go away.

And the weird thing is, that feeling was validated for me several times through the years. Call it a self-fulfilling prophecy if you want. But I did have a couple friends (at different times and periods of my life) that did "drift away" after they seemingly got tired of me.

Now, of course, the truth was probably much more about their own issues and what was going on in their lives, than it was me. But, each time, it felt like the world was just confirming what I already knew - I wasn't enough.

Eventually, at age 30, I met a guy who I thought I would marry. We hit it off immediately and our romance seemed to be something out of romance novels. We were head-over-heels for one another and everyone around us could see it too. It was like there was electricity in the air around us.

And for a little while, it was magical.

Until, it wasn't.

After about six months of being together, his behavior started to change and he began to be emotionally abusive. Then later, it became physically abusive as well.

It was a confusing time and is a topic that is so much more complex than I could explain on these few pages, but I know now, looking back, that one of the main reasons I stayed with him (and probably even subconsciously chose him in the first place), is because I didn't feel like I deserved anything better.

I had, after all, sort of separated myself from "everyone else." I would watch videos online of couples having wonderful marriage proposals and magical wedding ceremonies and I'd tear up. So happy for them, but also knowing deep down that those kinds of things were for "them," not me.

It was again, just part of the "truth" that I lived with. It was sad and I didn't want it to be that way, but it didn't really feel like I had a choice.

But then, one day, God revealed something to me that would start to challenge that supposed "truth."

Even though I had been saved and known Jesus since I was 27, I didn't really get to know Him until almost ten years later. After going through a series of traumas including the abusive relationship and the death of both of my parents, I had ended up with an advanced case of adrenal fatigue.

My body felt like it was shutting down on me and little things like taking a shower or doing the laundry would wipe me out for the rest of the day. There was no magic pill or wonder shot to get better, I just had to make some serious lifestyle changes.

So, I started sleeping more, I cleaned up my diet, started taking vitamin supplements and I started spending more time outside. But, the biggest change was I started to spend more time with God. I knew a big part of healing your adrenals is to face the emotional stress you've been "stuffing" and I wanted to feel better, so I was all for it. I started spending hours at a time in my room talking to the Lord. Of course, He had been there with me all those years prior and I knew it. I had significant moments of the Holy Spirit taking over for me in times of crisis with my ex and when my mom was in the hospital at the end of her fight with cancer. But this... this was a whole new type of relationship with Him.

He became my refuge and my healer. He was like my father, my friend, and my counselor all rolled into one. I read devotions, prayed, and spent hours meditating and visualizing myself unloading all of my burdens at His feet. And, it was during one of those moments, that He revealed a powerful truth.

Ever since I was a little girl, I had been trying to find my worth in everyone around me instead of in Him. I was almost desperate for it, which resulted in a lifetime of striving.

In His gentle and loving way, God made it clear that I had been looking for worth in all the wrong places. I had been operating under the belief that if I just did the right things, said the right things, had the right things, then I'd be "enough."

Striving to be perfect.

Striving to win people over.

Striving to be enough.

I could look back and see how I had acted those feelings out many times over the years. Trying to win the "approval" of my father and my sister growing up. And how it had carried over into my friendships and other relationships.

But, thankfully, Christ showed me that this wasn't the way it was going to be anymore. There was new management in town.

In His gentle and loving way, God made it clear that I had been looking for worth in all the wrong places. I had been operating under the belief that if I just did the right things, said the right things, had the right things, then I'd be "enough."

But, it was an exhausting and futile effort because there was no real definition of the word "enough." It could change at a moment's notice depending on who I was around, how they were feeling and what was going on in their life.

Not to mention, the negative voice that lived in my head – who would one day tell me that I was too shy and quiet and I needed to be bolder. Only to berate me the next time I spoke up for being too loud.

It was an impossible battle. I was set up for failure from the very start. Which is just what the enemy wanted. But there was one thing the enemy didn't account for. One thing he hoped I'd never realize. I am enough. Just the way I am.

My worth isn't determined by other people's opinions of me. It's not even determined by how well I perform or how nice of a person I am.

My worth comes from Him. Period.

I was wonderfully and fearfully made (Psalm 139:14) by the Lord Himself. He knew me before He even formed me in my mother's womb (Psalm 139:13). So, I am worthy because HE says I am. I am enough because HE says I am.

As Christ walked me through these truths and helped me remember who I really was in Him, it's like old scales fell from me. Chains were broken and veils were lifted.

It was actually so much simpler than I had been making it all those years.

I don't have to be perfect because HE is perfect.

I don't have to try to earn approval or prove my worth to the outside world because HE already approves of me, loves me, and knows my worth.

I am enough, because I am IN Christ.

Of course, it's difficult to hold on to this truth all the time. In a world of constant comparison and validation on social media, it's easy to get caught up in other people's opinions or in comparing your life to theirs and wondering if yours is enough.

But, in those moments, I focus on a visual that God showed me in my mind one day. In it, I saw myself walking amongst other people (both that I knew and didn't know) and each of us had a "beam" going from the top of our heads up to God. We each had our own individual beam and they didn't cross one another. They just always stayed perfectly straight and upright, between each one of us and God.

He was reminding me that each one of us is on our own unique path. Each one of us has our own unique purpose, gifting and talents. We will still be around others and we may even work with them or be encouraged by them, but nothing will ever alter that beam between us and God.

Our worth doesn't come from those around us. It only comes from above. And when we remember this, when we can really, truly accept that into our hearts, it's like the weight of the world comes off our shoulders. Because after all, like Jesus tells us in Matthew 11:30, His yoke is easy and His burden is light.

So, it's time to let go of all that weight you've been carrying, my friend. Set it down.

Because you ARE enough. Just as you are.

For Free

BY CARLA WARD

I was comprised of a fine, grey, powdery dust barely brushing against the concrete floor. I wasn't a whole being. I existed only as an array of monochromatic particulates that had carelessly attached themselves to each other in the shape of me. The fragments of my physical being had been pre-arranged at the base of a deep, dry, concrete block well. It was clean but colorless, with no variance in sheen or texture. I existed as particles of dust, not even a solid being.

Thirty feet above me, the faint daylight angled from the upper right of the round opening at ground level, down onto the left inside edge of the tunneled wall below. I couldn't turn my head or even guide my eyes toward the origin of the light because I wasn't arranged there with enough substance to create movement. I existed but I was not alive. I opened my eyelids as tiny slits, just enough that I could sense the presence of light. With my eyes focused on the floor to ensure I would not be distracted by a craving for life, the source of the frosted light was beyond my view.

Perhaps it was there so that I might be found one day, but not for me to achieve on my own. I was a shadow, not the light. My only purpose was to exist with the least possible amount of effort to sustain my breathing, or I would risk disintegration. The particles of my being would float away. Planning the intricacies of my next inhale was both the bare minimum engagement required to sustain me and was also the very threat to my existence.

The slightest error of creating movement would disrupt my dust particles. I didn't feel frightened that I was lying alone at the bottom of a deep well or that I might never be found in this unknown location. My sole focus was controlling with perfection the evenly patterned rise and fall of my lungs, that any movement would scatter the dust and I would cease to exist. There was no sound – the very movement of airwaves would have rearranged me. I didn't have enough space in my breathing to allow room to detect any scent. I was aware that the air was not fresh. I was likely only breathing in the very breath I had just exhaled.

There was no soul – just fragments of dust. My being was not complete enough to be afraid of existing. Surrendering my breath to its shallowest form was my only reason for taking up space at the center of a dry well floor. No one seeks dust. Certainly no one would notice dust in the shape of me thirty feet below the surface of the earth.

I rarely remember my dreams, but this was the first of three in 2010 that have rattled me to the extent that years later, I remember every detail. I didn't cry out in the middle of this one. I didn't ask for help or even have a thought that I should. I didn't even hear my own voice as I could give no attention to anything other than my controlled breathing. Nothing else would matter if I disintegrated as a result of not breathing properly. This dream in the well was the beginning of an awareness that I was failing to thrive. I thought that all I craved was the ability to breathe – the bare minimum existence. I would later learn that I was craving Freedom – the ability to flourish in the midst of crisis.

Failure to Thrive. It's a condition of newly born babies who suffer from arrested or downward physical growth and often results in abnormal development. They don't meet the recognized standards for growth. I couldn't grow less than the condition I was currently in. My soul was languishing. Worse was my fear that no one would notice. This manifested for me when I was at the height of my greatest pileup of fears. As it turns out, fear and freedom are in direct, and often devastating, competition with each other. Fear is a life-sucking, soul crushing, dream-killing thief. Fear and Freedom cannot co-exist.

Within just a few months of each other, most of my treasured relationships were crumbling. I was preparing to move out of the home my husband and I had designed and built. The marriage was broken beyond recognition and I suspected his office secretary was the reason he was not willing to partner with me to sustain it. During the same week of moving to a rental in a neighborhood where I knew no one, my son overdosed on heroin. I watched the paramedics carry my 6' 4" son's lifeless body down a set of stairs and into the ambulance. I would follow behind in a car with my estranged husband who had no support to offer me in this crisis. My son survived and was released from the hospital after three nights of intensive care. He was escorted from the hospital in handcuffs and shackles and taken immediately to prison, where he would spend the next three years of his life. Within three weeks, my father had become gravely ill as a result of complications from a kidney transplant. He and my mother were living on the other side of the country. My oldest son had just lost his job and was raising his two young daughters on his own. My family was broken, and I had no idea how to support any of them. Additionally, I had unwittingly signed up for a crash course in drug addition, manipulating the prison system, and launching a divorce. I had been sucked into a tornado, dropped in a distant field, and left there with crippling fears that separated my soul from my body. My fear of my circumstances had convinced me that Freedom would never be mine to achieve.

I had been a Christian since I was a child. I was raised in a fantastic family that believed in God, was service-focused, and was very active in church. I was a Christian. I met the requirements and could check all the boxes. We were a church-focused family. Yet, I have no memory of ever talking about Jesus as my Savior. If we had a bible in our home, I don't recall knowing of it.

The world teaches us to create dream lists, vision boards and bucket lists. These are great tools to set goals and pursue big ambitions. My vision included being actively involved in the tasks of the church. But I did not know who Jesus is for me. Worse, I didn't even know that I was supposed to know. The picture of my life was now leaking out of its frame and I was fragile beyond the point of recognizing myself in the mirror, in my relationships, in my life. My self-sufficient self was now languishing. I had become so riddled with fear that my identity had become rooted in it. There was no space in my head for even the thought of flourishing freedom.

Fear quickly invaded my sleep. The very thing that was supposed to be my respite had now been infected by fear. I would wake up in the middle of the night gasping for air. The dreams that I remembered revolved around breathing, either not getting enough oxygen or desperately trying to inhale so shallowly that my breath could not cause my dust particles to dissipate. I craved healing and knew that I did not have the capacity to do this on my own. Self-sufficiency had failed me, and I needed help.

I began attending a local church that I'd driven past many times. It was big, well-resourced and rooted in Jesus. Big mattered to me because I did not want to be noticed. I wanted to slide into church each week and leave again unnoticed. I had nothing to give any one and I had barely enough stamina to show up each week. But I did show up – every single Sunday. I became so hungry for God that I became a desperate student seeking wisdom. I studied every sermon and filled out the sermon notes each week. Then I took them home and studied them again. I began going to bible studies and attended very faithfully. I didn't previously understand that I was hungry for Jesus – and that He, too was hungering for me. I was unaware that Jesus was preparing me for my first steps toward freedom.

In God's economy, He equips us to thrive. His goal for us is flourishing freedom, which glorifies Him. Glorifying God is our single purpose in life. I was not thriving, I was existing, and poorly at that. But the nuance is that the flourishing – fruit bearing – is not for us to produce. That's God's privilege. Instead He calls us to sink our roots deep in the soil (His Word) and abide by the river (His Son) where we have been planted (Jeremiah 17:5-8). When we are obedient to this relationship, God begins to produce the fruit in us. Only by the work of Jesus Christ do we begin to evolve from languishing to flourishing. From the imprisonment of self-sufficiency, our identity as the child of the King releases us to the freedom of a flourishing soul. It requires a Savior to transform fear into freedom.

When God used Jeremiah to speak to the exiles in Babylon, Jeremiah advised them of God's plan to keep them captive for 70 years. Imagine the potential for fear to creep in during seven decades of captivity! God wanted them to be assured that He would not forget them and that he would ultimately bring them home. Jeremiah 29:11 is one of the better-known scriptures because we cling to the promise of flourishing freedom, "...to give you a future and a hope". What often is overlooked however, when God makes a promise is that it often comes with an instruction. In this case, before God made the promise to prosper the captives, He instructed them to hunker down – to settle into the place where He planted them. In Jeremiah 29:5-7 God's instruction that preceded the prosperity promise was to establish their homes and plan to stay, handle their responsibilities, and grow their families. He confirmed their exile and instructed them to pray for Babylon. The welfare of the city where they were held captive would determine their personal welfare, and therefore their personal freedom.

Were they afraid? Yes! Were they disappointed to have been located here for such a long duration? Yes! But God promised that their future well-being and freedom would be completely dependent on their attentiveness to bringing to God their prayers for a flourishing city. Their future success would hinge on their commitment to settle in where God had planted them. God was instructing the captives to set aside their fears for their future and focus on their relationship with Him. It is the very nature of perfect love described in 1 John 4:18 that it casts out all fear and thus produces the freedom that a languishing soul craves.

One of the earliest truths I learned in my quest for overcoming my suffocating soul was the biblical truth about fear. I took a four-week class based on Max Lucado's book, "Fearless". (How did God know to provide this topic at the precise time I needed it most? This idea of God's perfect timing would become a prevailing theme for me as my walk with Jesus evolved and grew.) I began to understand that my son was not the only prisoner in our family. Fear had been holding me captive because I didn't understand its presence and worse, its power over me. Lucado says, "Fear herds us into a prison and slams the doors."

My unchecked fears may as well have dressed me in drab green Wisconsin inmate garb, assigned me a six-digit DOC number, and thrown me into solitary confinement. It was 1 John 4:18 where I camped out, trying to absorb the truth that perfect love casts out all fear. He doesn't say that human love (which is imperfect) casts out fear. He says that perfect love casts out fear. Perfect love is only of God. Jesus was the only human to know perfect love. While we strive to love more fully and deeply, our earthly hearts can only receive perfect love. We cannot give it because of sin.

The other critical truth in this passage is that perfect love doesn't just cast out some fear, it casts out all fear. All fear. How could I ever achieve the complete absence of fear? Lucado eloquently reminds us, "It is not the absence of storms that sets us apart. It's whom we discover in the storm: An unstirred Christ."

I began to visualize fear and love as separate balloons in a container. If I had any fear at all, we're taught in 1 John 4:18 that it is out of fear of punishment. And that the only antidote for fear is perfect love. I began to visualize my love for Jesus growing, expanding, never bursting, always prevailing. The fear balloon in the container, by its very powerlessness, had no option but to shrink. The very practice of knowing, loving and evolving in my relationship with Jesus automatically (as He promised) diminished my fears. In essence, perfect love and fear cannot coexist in the same relationship. Because God IS perfect love, I never have to walk in fear. I never have to accept fear as my default.

Loving Christ and receiving the perfection of his love produces a flourishing soul. Love is the very weapon to cast out fear, which ultimately is where we find true freedom. But how do we do that?

Learning to trust that Jesus is who He says He is means that I don't have to be anything more than the Father created me to be. My worth and my identity are not dependent on the next crisis in my life or my ability to surrender my fears and failures. I don't have to see into the future to predict the well-being of my loved ones. I don't have to carry anger or hatred over a husband who walked away from our marriage. Knowing my identity as a chosen, beloved, sanctified child of a King means I never again see myself as fragmented particles on the floor of a deep, desolate well.

*"As it turns out, fear and freedom are in direct,
and often devastating, competition with each other.
Fear is a life sucking, soul-crushing, dream-killing thief."*

Jesus doesn't require me to know everything about Him in order to be loved by Him. I can hand over my self-sufficiency to the One who is fully and completely sufficient. He who is Love loves me perfectly, which leaves no room for fear. "Listen all you people... This is what the Lord says: Do not be afraid. Do not be discouraged by this mighty army, for the battle is not yours, but God's." 2 Chronicles 20:15. The battle is God's and He has already won.

I am in Him and He is in me. I am not the shadow. I am the light. All flourishing occurs in the light. Freedom expands in direct proportion to the pursuit of perfect love. I am free! And the good news is so are you! Scripture References: NLT

*"Freedom expands in direct proportion
to the pursuit of perfect love."*

True Freedom Comes Through Forgiveness

BY CARRIE REICHARTZ

Do you want to know the secret for finding true freedom? You may not like it, but the number one success to getting out of life struggles and finding true freedom is ...drumroll please... forgiveness.

Can it be that simple, and then just forgive everyone and don't take offense of situations, you will be free from struggles. Yeah, right! Easier said than done. Are we willing to trust God?

God's Word teaches us about forgiveness. Let's debunk some myths regarding forgiveness that are keeping us stuck. I will share two stories of grave forgiveness in my life - sexual abuse and rape and a Christian mentor and leader that rejected and betrayed me. Then let's come together and study further Biblical examples that if you follow will allow you to live with a life follow in after God instead of living a life stuck in bitterness.

WHAT IS FORGIVENESS?

Forgiveness is letting go of the desire to pass judgment on a situation or a person that has wronged you and allowing God's love to flow in and heal you. By letting God's love come in and heal you, you are freeing yourself to live your full life.

I know; I know, you might say: "But you don't know what they did to me. They are spreading rumors and lies about me. They sexually abused me. They took advantage of me financially and I am ruined. Horrible things have happened to me." The list could go on and on. Before Christ came into my life, I thought the same things.

I realize and sympathize. It is hard. I've had to forgive similar things in my life. However, holding onto the hurt, whatever the hurt, is not helping you. Whatever you are stewing about is not hurting the person that hurt you at all. It is hurting you.

Some say forgiveness is a "get-out-of-jail-free card". That is true, but not for the person you think. Forgiveness doesn't let the people off who have done wrong. People are accountable to God. He will handle those people and situations. God is the only one who can truly judge their actions. They are not getting out of jail free; YOU are.

Forgiveness actually lets you off. You are not responsible for watching them, complaining about them, or enforcing the "rules" over them. You give that responsibility over to God and it frees you. By releasing this to God, YOU get out of a jail that you held yourself in by holding onto bitterness, resentment, blame, anger, complaining and revenge.

Do you want free and total freedom?
If so, you must walk the road of forgiveness

That freed space in your mind leaves room in your life for other things: more of God's love, His calling, and the purpose He has for you. When you are stuck enforcing the rules on someone else or reliving it and complaining, you are not available for those things.

Think of it like the hard drive on your computer. If space is taken up with programs and files not being used, you don't have room for the important stuff you do need to use. Your hard drive has a lot more extra space for unusable information than your life does. Don't allow wasted thoughts, feelings, and emotions to take up the space God wants to use to love you and lead you in the direction He has for you.

Forgiveness frees up your life for amazing things. Do you want to have that amazing life today?

DEBUNKING MYTHS

Forgiveness is not getting back into a relationship with someone. Forgiveness means letting go of the desire to "get back," blame, or wallow in self-pity about what someone did to you or a situation. It may be best for you not to be in a relationship with that person and that does not mean you haven't forgiven them. It is our heart toward God that we need to watch, not the other person and our physical closeness with them.

Forgiving doesn't mean forgetting. The situation or person will keep coming to mind for a while and that is okay and normal. Forgiveness is shown when the situation or person comes to our mind and we ask ourselves, 'what do we do with it?' Do we dwell on it and turn it over and over in our minds or do we let it go and remind ourselves that God will take care of it? We cannot allow ourselves to be distracted from living a full life for God and ourselves by focusing our life focused on other people or a situation.

"They don't deserve forgiveness for what they did." That may very well be true; they probably don't deserve it. But this is inherent in the definition of forgiveness. If the person being forgiven deserved it, it would not be labeled forgiveness. Forgiveness always goes to those who don't deserve it.

Remember, we do not deserve forgiveness either but we receive it. Therefore, no matter the situation, we need to forgive. This need is about us, not the other person or the situation. Forgiving sets us free from personally holding them accountable for their actions. Forgiveness leaves it up to God to handle the situation. Forgiveness leaves us free for wonderful works and a shiny new life, untainted by the actions or inactions of others, because we are full of His love.

It's great to hear all this and be reminded of what forgiveness is and/or isn't, but without real-life examples of how someone forgives, it is hard to know how to apply it in our lives. Let me share just two of my own life examples that required difficult forgiveness.

SEXUAL ABUSE

My early years of life were not easy. During the first five years of my life I was sexually abused. Then, from age 11-13, I was repeatedly sexually assaulted and raped. These events ruled my life. Fear and self-protection were my baseline for everything. I didn't know a life any different other than being completely full of fear. It wasn't until I was 30 that I even admitted to anyone these events happened and then fully saw how much they ruled my life. They were making me physically, mentally, emotionally, and spiritually sick in so many ways. The years of abuse were still driving my daily life and I didn't even know it. Please read my book "I Just Want My Life Back: From Trauma to Triumph" for more on this story.

When I was working through forgiveness on the trauma that was inflicted upon me during my formative and teenage years, the people responsible were not alive. So, I sat down and wrote each person that abused me an individual letter. Even though it was painful, I wrote a forgiveness letter to them. It helped me work through deep seated pain and come to freedom.

First, I wrote down all my hurt and pain. To name just a few: isolation it left me in, fear, not being the wife and mom I wanted to be, later life situations it led me into, people-pleasing, the list went on and on.

Then I acknowledged my part in that pain. You did this to me, but I chose to hide it. I chose not to tell anyone.
I acknowledged that they were probably hurt in their childhoods in similar ways, which brought them to doing these acts.

I expressed forgiveness for them. "I let you go from my mind and body. I wish to move forward in my life; free and forgiven for my mistakes. Therefore, I am forgiving you."

After I wrote these letters, I burned them. That represented my letting go of the situation and the people and letting God handle it.

POWER OF FORGIVENESS

I worked through this forgiveness process with God and after many years, He called me to open a center in Kenya that helps teen girls that are pregnant as a result of rape and sexual abuse. All the miracles and workings of God that have occurred in this process cannot even be contained in a book. I got to experience those because I chose to forgive. Had I remained in hurt, pain, and anger, God wouldn't have been able to work through me to do this. We need to be willing; He will do the rest. God does bring beauty from ashes, but we need to allow Him to help us with the work of forgiveness in the middle of that.

CHRISTIAN LEADER BETRAYAL/REJECTION

In my fifth year of walking with Christ, a Christian leader/ mentor, that I had based my walk after, asked me to help start a non-profit. I prayed and felt the Lord leading me. She was the founder and executive director. I did the legal work to obtain the 501(c)(3) tax status. During that process, we got deep into what the project would look like and she asked me to be the board President. I accepted. I worked hard day and night to get the nonprofit to the next level, doing whatever was asked of me and coming up with ideas to pursue. I worked 10-15 hours a day on this project for several months.

I was doing most of the work along with my mentor. The rest of the board was doing very little. Even the little work they volunteered to do at meetings rarely got done. Four months in, I was going out of the country for ten days. When I returned, I was asked to leave the board because "people were complaining about me".

My heart and soul, my hard work and effort were in this organization and she is asking me to leave?

She knew how hard I worked, we had worked together. She also knew and complained about how the rest of the board was doing nothing and now she's asking ME to leave! After all I did to help her and this project! I'm the only one helping her. I felt betrayed.

I was emotionally devastated. It hit me to my core. She was my spiritual example and mentor. My best was not good enough for her and the board. They didn't want any part of me. I was rejected and abandoned by them even after all my hard work and efforts.

I poured myself into this organization and had given my all to it for months. I was kicked to the curb, left by the side of the road, with accusations, which, to this day, I still do not know what they were. On top of that, people did not handle the situation as the Bible would have called them to. Instead they threw me under the bus without any discussion or self-examination. How unfair! How ungodly! How ungrateful!

I knew God would want me to forgive, but it hurt so badly.

I remember during those moments right after the conversation, there was a minute-by-minute process of forgiveness. It was constantly on my mind and in my heart. The lies said about me, my wanting to point out the unbiblical way this was being handled. The hurt was so deep. This was a Christian leader, someone who had brought me close to God for the first time in my life. How could she, of all people, do this to me?

How could I have invested so much and then be left out?
I didn't understand and it felt not right and it hurt.

One of the things that I vowed to myself and God was that I was not going to pull this organization or the people involved in the mud with me. As much as I wanted to, and from my perspective, they deserved it, I knew that was not what God wanted. It was hard not to talk about the situation. It was consuming my mind, but I did not go on about it.

I had two Christian friends that I would vent to, but that was it. I would not talk about it with anyone else. It was hard, but within a few days and weeks of my solid commitment to quietness, it got a lot easier. The thoughts came through my mind a little less often – maybe once an hour instead of once a minute. As time passed, it was less and less on my mind because I made a choice not to entertain those thoughts but chose other ones.

POWER OF FORGIVENESS

By keeping my mouth shut about what they did wrong, God was able to show me what I had to learn from the situation. First, I realized I did not pray about taking on the position of President in this organization. God had called me to help them with the legal work of getting started and I accepted the appointment through excitement, but without prayer. Second, the work with that organization was distracting me from the Kenya work God was calling me to do. If I was focused solely on them and "what they did to me," I would never have seen my part in this and learn my lessons.

"God does bring beauty from ashes, but we need to allow Him to help us with the work of forgiveness in the middle of that."

If we don't forgive, we are walking on dangerous ground. Whatever measuring stick we use against others to judge whether or not they should be forgiven is the same stick that God will use against us. The Lord's Prayer (Matthew 6:9-13 & Luke 11:2-4) tells us He will forgive us the same way as we forgive others.

If we honestly examine ourselves, we know we need to have liberal forgiveness from God and others for things we know we have done wrong and for things we don't even realize we have done wrong. Therefore, we better be offering that same forgiveness standard to others. If we do not, we won't be given those same liberal standards from God of forgiveness either. Don't let pride keep you from all God has for you. Unforgiveness is a form of pride. Don't stay stuck there. Forgiveness leads to freedom and leaves God in charge of judging other people's actions. Since forgiveness was bought with the precious blood of Jesus Christ, who better to be the judge of other people's behaviors?

With these examples, I hope you are willing to realize that it doesn't matter what has been done to you. Forgiveness is the only way out of the situation and struggle. I know it's hard, painful, and feels unfair. But with God it is possible and it is the only way to be set free. God will punish what needs to be punished and He will love us through the hurt you can rest in that.

HOW DO YOU FORGIVE?
Here are some specific actions that can help with forgiveness.

Look to God, through the Bible, for emotional healing. His word will heal your hurting heart if you allow it to. Prayer. Pray about what makes you angry, sad, and hurt. Take these things to God and share your feelings with Him. Journal. Write a forgiveness letter, prayers, or draw or create. Be careful who you share your heart with. Make sure they're a spiritual friend. Share with a limited number of people. Don't allow yourself to talk about it all the time. Go to God – that is the only place you will find lasting healing. Look at the other person's perspective. People rarely purposefully hurt us. Try to see the other person's view of the situation even if you don't agree with it. Remember times when you hurt people and were forgiven. Look at your part. Maybe we trusted someone that should not have been trusted. Maybe we are involved in something we should not be involved with. Look for lessons to bring with you.

Remember, forgiving does not mean forgetting. Please do not set yourself up for unreasonable expectations. You do not need to

79

forget the situation ever happened. Forgiveness means you commit to changing your thoughts about the situation or person. You commit to not letting the situation or person control you anymore. When it comes into your mind, you choose to let it flow right back out of your mind instead of stewing over it.

FORGIVENESS LETTER
Write a letter to whoever wronged you:

Explain all your hurt and pain. Get all the details and feelings out. Admit your part in that pain. Express how things might look different from their perspective.
Express forgiveness for them "Because of what Jesus did for me, I let you go from my mind and body. I wish to move forward in my life, free and forgiven for my mistakes. Therefore, I am forgiving you."
Burn, rip, or throw the letter in the ocean.
This represents letting go of the situation or person and letting God handle it.
It is no longer your problem to solve or burden to carry.

Do not give the letter to the person under any circumstances. This letter is about forgiveness for you. It is not about them. They don't need to know anything about it. Consult with a trusted spiritual advisor if you need further help with this.

BIBLICAL EXAMPLES OF FREEDOM/FORGIVENESS
Continue your study by slowly going through these:

Joseph - forgiving his brothers and false allegations against him in Genesis, Chapters 37-50

David - self-forgiveness; moving on after bad decisions II Samuel 11-12

Lord's Prayer - "Father forgive us our sins as I forgive those who sin against me." Matthew 6:9-15

Jesus - on the cross forgiving all the Jews and Romans. Luke 23:34

Stephen - forgiving the men stoning him to death in Acts 7:54- and on "...love the Lord your God with all your heart, mind, & strength." Deuteronomy 6:5

WHY IS FORGIVENESS IMPORTANT?

Lack of forgiveness blocks our way to God. It is always in the way. Even if we don't consciously think about it often, it is there like a pebble, rock or boulder blocking the river of God's purposes for you. After a while, with enough boulders and pebbles, the river stops flowing. There is a ton of pressure built up behind the rock, which can lead to anger, self-medicating, physical and emotional illnesses and symptoms, and so many other things. The worst part is, you can't be in God's love, purpose and flow for your life if bitterness, resentment, and lack of forgiveness are blocking the river. We need to let go of the rocks and then the flow of God will return to us. We need to let go of the lack of forgiveness no matter what the situation. Then we can be free to move forward with God.

Are you ready to be in the love and flow of God again? Take some time today to start working through your pebbles and boulders of unforgiveness and see the love of God return like a tidal wave into your life. You bring the willingness and He will bring the miracles!

Healed to Serve

BY DAWN SUEHRING

My story is one of living a fairytale, experiencing devastation, simply going through the motions of living, healing, and through God's abundant blessings coming through life's storms a healthier, more positive and truly blessed woman. God's healing brought me closer to Him in service to Him and people halfway around the world.

The start of my life was very blessed. I was born the first of five children to loving parents. I was raised in a small town in a safe and comfortable environment. My childhood was much like a fairytale – doted on by parents and grandparents; close connections with aunts, uncles and cousins; regular church attendance; little white dresses with lace and ribbons, hand-made by my grandma and, of course, no outfit was complete without 'ruffle butt' panties and hand sewn lace on my socks. I grew up as the caring, responsible eldest sibling; studied diligently in school; enjoyed all things musical; and especially loved being around and caring for babies and young children. God's grace of being born into a loving family, being born the first of five children and living in a country where there is freedom of religion were all things out of my control. This surrounded me, as well as my close extended family ties, my love for music, my overall sense of comfort and safety brought me great happiness.

Life is a journey. A compilation of events and circumstances all around us. Some things happen TO us, while other things require some degree of participation. The majority of people would likely say they preferred a life full of contentment, happiness and blessings rather than one of struggles, anxiety, anger and sadness. The truth is, an individual's life is made up of a multitude of emotions, positive and negative, experienced in a variety of circumstances.

As human beings we often desire some degree of control in our life's circumstances. As Christians we desire the certainty that our path will lead to heaven. The control we have is to seek God in order to have a relationship with Him. The Bible tells us to

"Love the Lord your God with all your heart and with all your soul and with all your strength." Deuteronomy 6:5 (NIV)

We are to LOVE God. Loving is active. It is ongoing. We are tasked with doing these things that God wants. Loving God means loving your neighbor also. Through love we are bound together, extending our hearts to God.

We all experience times of sadness, anxiety, anger and ill-fortune. But as I grew and learned to lean into and trust Christ Jesus my struggles, negative thoughts and experiences, fear and self-doubt began to diminish. Even in our darkest moments God's light can shine, turning our circumstances around, working our struggles for good, teaching us necessary lessons and ultimately blessing us in his favor. We need only SEEK HIM and grow our personal relationship with God. By changing our thoughts, words and actions we begin to speak and act as God would have us do. Our relationship with God must come first: spending time in the Word, Praying to God our Father, and treating others with the love and respect of our Lord and Savior bring us peace and healing through these hard times. God has blessed me with healing throughout my life. Through the devastation of a failed first marriage, through betrayal as a wife and partner, through my many fears (fear of not being enough - in relationships, as a parent, a friend and family member and in the search for a new job) He has stood by me, strengthened me, loved me for ME and brought healing to my heart and in my life.

Ephesians teaches those of us who believe how we are to live as followers of Jesus, how to be victorious in our spiritual battles, and who we are in Christ. We learn that we are loved unconditionally and infinitely without end. And this is where we find true healing. God heals His people so that His people heal others. He pours His grace on us in order that we may pour it over onto those without hope so they can hope again after our stories of Him healing us.

"I pray that your hearts will be flooded with light so that you can understand the confident hope he has given to those he called – his holy people who are his rich and glorious inheritance"
Ephesians 1:18 (NIV)

Transitioning to adulthood can be challenging. Through hard work and perseverance, my goal of becoming a Registered Nurse was pursued and achieved. Since babies were my passion, I sought a job working in Neonatal Intensive Care. Having found my 'dream career', I reveled in the fact that I truly LOVED the path I was on because I was able to use my God-given knowledge and skills to heal little babies and bring healing to their parents' hearts as well.

I married at the age of 25. Over the next year I became the mother of a beautiful baby girl. I was living my dream life – mommy of this incredible daughter, successful career, future goals in mind. I strongly desired to advance my career and to become an Advanced Practice Nurse in neonatology. During the intensive year of school, I was not allowed to work (thus, a financial burden for my family); I was still a mother and a wife (bringing emotional struggles as well as time constraints and exhaustion). Thankful for my youth and blessed with strength and healing that came from trusting in the Lord, I pushed onward. Through tears of exhaustion, challenges in childcare and feelings that I was falling short (not 'enough') in providing the desired attention to my baby and husband, I persevered. I graduated and passed my national certification and continued on my merry way. Life was good for a while. We were well off financially, fulfilled in our jobs, and we added two incredible sons to our family.

I loved the concept of being married... Having come from a family, my parents as well as immediate family (uncles, aunts and grandparents) who remained married to the same partner their entire lives I wanted and EXPECTED a similar experience in my life. Somehow, I always knew how I was SUPPOSED to feel in my relationship with my husband; a loving and equal partnership; amicable discussions to resolve issues; feeling loved even in my weakness.

The problem I ran into repeatedly was that I didn't always feel that way... In fact, as the years passed, and I continued to 'fix' things and 'make excuses' for his behavior and why things weren't as I had believed they would be, my life began to unravel. There had been, through the years, many 'red flags' (my husband's drinking to excess, the tone of his voice and harsh words for me at times, his minimal interest in participating in activities related to our precious children). I realized that not only was I the caretaker of three young children but of my husband as well.

But true to my nature I remained the nurturing, caring, 'do whatever it takes' wife and mother... the 'fix it' girl always turning the less desirable situations into a more positive version, determined I would succeed at this marriage thing. Life was good, at times but there were many extremely dark and painful times filled with deep sadness and betrayal. Unfortunately, my husband's reality of the commitment necessary in marriage didn't quite match up to my own level of commitment.

In June of 2005, after nearly 22 years of marriage, my world, as I knew it, crumbled around me. I found myself an abandoned 46-year-old, devastated single mother of 15 and 16-year-old sons and a 19-year-old daughter pregnant with our first grandchild. WHO WAS I NOW? I had 'worked the plan', done things the 'right way' only to find myself and my teenage children abandoned. At a time in my life where my faith typically would have offered me solace, I experienced despair.

"I have come into the world as a light, so that no one who believes in me should stay in darkness." John 12:46 (NIV)

Even the most devout Christians falter. I was no different as I moved through life working, mothering and living, I did not pay attention to filling my mind and heart with the Word of the Lord. I neglected regular attendance at church. I forgot about praying regularly. My positivity and zest for life gradually faded. I needed the biggest healing yet.

Overtime, I realized that through God's divine intervention combined with our action, He uses our trials to build up our faith and strengthens our personal relationship with Him. Through the love and grace of our Lord Jesus Christ and the unconditional love and support of my parents, extended family, friends and my three children, I managed to slowly climb from the depths of despair. My depression gradually lifted; My anxiety and panic attacks softened; I reevaluated my life, my living arrangements, my goals, my purpose.

First and foremost, I needed to restore my relationship with God in my life as number one priority. After that I needed to guide my children through that same process as best I could. The healing process took a tremendous amount of work and attention to medical, psychological, emotional, and spiritual ailment. My children and I survived, coming through the lowest of times as stronger individuals and stronger as a family. Only through the limitless love of God and our conscious actions to renew our relationship with God were we able to return to a place of healing, feeling blessed, and it was time to start being a more consistent blessing to others.

"Blessed is the one who perseveres under trial because, having stood the test, that person will receive the crown of life that the Lord has promised to those who love him." James 1:12 (NIV)

Mission work was always a dream I had entertained from

early in my adult life. I enjoyed traveling and felt that combining my wanderlust spirit and offering my medical training gifts would be exciting, fulfilling, and means to serve others. I felt that my profession as well as my personality and caring nature were well-suited for mission work and that God would lead me down that path when the time was right. After finding healing through Jesus and redefining myself in Him and not in myself, following my divorce and being established within my profession, I began to feel a stronger calling in my heart. I prayed for guidance in timing for a mission trip, a location to serve, as well as finances to accomplish this venture.

*"Life is a journey.... Some things happen TO us,
while other things require some degree of participation."*

In 2016 I was participating in a fundraising event for Operation Give Hope which does medical and other mission work in Kenya. I reconnected with several women and was invited on a medical mission trip to Kenya. God had placed me in exactly the right place at the right time, and I couldn't have been more thrilled for this opportunity. I embraced the experience and moved forward with positivity and excitement.

I was only able to do this because of the healing I allowed God to work in my heart. The well-known story in the Bible of the priest, the Pharisee and the Samaritan who each come upon the man who had been traveling from Jerusalem to Jericho and fell victim to an attacker - beaten, robbed and left for dead on the side of the road exemplifies the Lord's love and compassion. God is the ultimate Samaritan. When we are down trodden by life's challenges; just trying to get by, God gives us grace, love and compassion.

On that trip, despite the labor-intensive grind of our duties and the phenomenal heat and humidity, I felt empowered and wanted to continue to help the Kenyan people in whatever ways my talents could "Life is a journey... Some things happen TO us, while other things require some degree of participation." be used. I went on my second mission trip in 2017, equally as enthused before, during and following our trip.

Since that time, I work with Infinitely More Life and Mercy's Light Family continuing my Kenya connection. Currently my work is supporting pregnant teens, babies, and our Kenyan staff. I educate them in personal hygiene, care of their newborns and their baby's desired developmental milestones and many other areas. I also work with the local medical clinic and provide training in helping babies breathe, hand-washing and other important nursing topics. To date I've been to Kenya five times and also work hard in the US for funding, planning, and education. My plan, God willing is to continue to provide support, provided I am an effective member of the team and God continues to call me to serve.

I have learned so much from my Kenyan family and friends – joy is simple, as long as you BELIEVE in God! When there are struggles, all we need to do is PRAY!! I continue to be in awe of the degree of FAITH the Kenyan people have – they may lack financial security, what we may consider a safe dwelling place, supplies we take for granted to make ourselves and our children's lives more comfortable BUT THEY EXUDE SUPREME FAITH IN JESUS CHRIST and the Lord's eternal beauty shines through their eyes!!! Seeing their trust in Jesus in very difficult circumstances has brought another level of emotional and spiritual healing to me that I didn't even know was possible! Yes... I am truly BLESSED... through Jesus' healing and you can be too!

I am Healthy

BY ANGELA MAGER

The story of my health evolution mirrors the transformation of my identity. It began when my confidence was suddenly wrecked in the first grade. That was the year I participated in a dance contest. When I loved dancing and performing. It amazes me that I had the courage to get up in front of all my peers that day.

There was a large rowdy crowd of kids, the entire first grade. We were all packed into two classrooms connected by an open accordion partition. About ten of us competed in the contest, while the other students sat cross-legged on the floor.

I don't remember the song we danced to, but it was the disco era. It was likely either Donna Summer or The Village People. I danced my heart out. Twirling and shimmying, waving my pigtails in time with the music. Given the many accolades I'd received while performing in front of parents and grandparents at home, I was sure I was the best of the group. In my mind, I would be the obvious winner.

Afterward, the students were all instructed to vote on slips of paper. For a moment, I contemplated if it was wrong to vote for myself. Then with a smile, I printed my own name in large block letters. I was sure my vote would be only one of many, many others.

As the names of the winners were being called, I prepared myself. I was ready to jump to my feet and accept the congratulations upon hearing my name. But it never happened. I sat in stunned silence as the class clown bounded forward for his first-place prize. "How did he win?" I wondered to myself, "He wasn't dancing. He was just being silly."

The teacher at the front of the room announced that the teachers had voted, too. As I heard my name announced, I stood with a sense of vindication. Receiving the award of honorable mention from those kind souls momentarily lifted my spirits. But it was an empty feeling, knowing I wasn't chosen by the official critics.

Everything became a blur, as I sat holding my blue construction paper ribbon. The disappointment was clearly reflected in my expression. A teacher seated nearby looked down at me with pity. That day, rejected by my peers in such a public way, I learned it's preferable to stay hidden rather than risk getting hurt.

That's the first memory I have of the unhealthy self-image that developed. I became more conscious of my appearance, comparing myself to the other girls. Although I was a healthy size by anyone's standards, I worried that my legs were too fleshy. I hated my frizzy hair, my plain features, and the dark hair on my arms and legs. From that day forward, I tried to fit in or blend in. And my favorite tactic, to be as invisible as possible.

After school I often sought solace in sweet snacks. It became a habit to eat cookie dough by the spoonful standing in front of the refrigerator. I recognize now, that was the start of the abdominal bloating, and dizzy spells. In 9th grade I had my first fainting spell one early morning.

I was stirring a pitcher of OJ from concentrate, when I began to see stars and the room became black. Luckily, I set the glass pitcher down before I crashed on the linoleum while my mom watched helplessly across the room. As I came back to consciousness, I noticed the panic in her voice before the pain in my head. The planned day at the beach was thwarted for a trip to the doctor instead. The only suggestion he could offer, after a quick exam and some blood work, was to increase my iron intake.

At the same time, I dealt with insecurity from a preoccupation with thoughts of myself. I became convinced that everyone I encountered was evaluating me. How I looked, how I acted, how dumb I sounded if I ventured to join a conversation. My self-esteem was wholly based on what I presumed others thought of me. And I imagined the worst.

Those fears dictated the clothes I wore, and who I was willing to approach. They kept me from speaking up in class. I was always diligent about my grades. For that reason, I bemoaned the injustice when participation was a percentage of the final average. I would rather take the hit in the grade book than raise my hand. And group assignments struck fear to my core.

Burdened by these insecurities, I began to seek Jesus when I was in high school. I was invited to a youth revival at a classmate's church. There was live music, pizza, and a prevalent feeling of inclusion. The group was friendly and seemed genuine in their welcoming reception. It was exhilarating, and I wanted more of that sense of acceptance.

I continued to visit churches, trying to recapture the experience. However, I never felt that same heartfelt recognition at a Sunday morning service. By the time I realized that, though, my aim had shifted. It grew into a yearning to know Jesus.

I credit much of my deepening faith to a teacher I worked with early in my career when I had the joy of being an elementary school nurse. She shared wonderful devotional books with me, encouraged my faith, and we had interesting theological discussions. She inspired me to begin memorizing scripture. That was also the time when my daily morning conversations with Jesus were birthed.

I was "setting my mind on things above, not on earthly things". Colossians 3:2 (NIV)

I was slowly changing. Becoming more secure in who I was – A new creation. "Therefore, if anyone is in Christ, he is a new creature; the old things passed away; behold, new things have come." 2 Corinthians 5:17.

At the end of my last year working at that school, a large group of young teachers decided to celebrate at a karaoke bar. The enthusiasm of their invitation compelled me to check it out. It was the early 90's, and I had never even heard of karaoke before. I wasn't sure what to expect. But I was delighted to be included.

We arrived early, and chose a table directly in front of the stage. As groups of three or four would perform songs together, it felt safe to join a few. We sang Lucky Star by Madonna, and Girls Just Wanna Have Fun by Cyndi Lauper.

Slowly, but surely, I was feeling more comfortable and by the end of the night, I was emboldened to sing a song all by myself. It was Brass in Pocket, by The Pretenders. Not content to only sing the song, I had to dance and pantomime the lyrics "I'm gonna use my arms, I'm gonna use my legs". I strutted on the stage as if I was Chrissie Hynde herself. All this without a single sip of alcohol.

Word got around the next day at school, how "Nurse Mager" let her hair down at karaoke. Strangely, I didn't care what anyone thought. I wasn't afraid of being rejected. I let the real me shine. That little girl who loved to sing and dance got to be free again!

Free of fear. Free of self-rejection.

"For God gave us a spirit not of fear but of power and love and self-control." 2 Timothy 1:7 (ESV)

Physical health is intricately connected to mental and spiritual health. As my thoughts aligned with biblical truths, my physical health was also positively affected.

"My renewed mind led to a transformation in life and health. From that day forward, I tried to fit in or blend in."

Cravings became easier to manage. Because dietary choices directly impact symptoms, I felt healthier. Dizziness, heart palpitations, and fainting spells vanished. Abdominal bloating and gas were dramatically reduced. Sleep became easier and less disturbed throughout the night.

I learned not to conform to the standard way of thinking, or of eating. My renewed mind led to a transformation in life and health.

"Do not be conformed to this world, but be transformed by the renewal of your mind, that by testing you may discern what is the will of God, what is good and acceptable and perfect." Romans 12:2 (ESV)

I still get nervous and uneasy at times. But my self-image is much healthier. I understand that everyone else is too busy dealing with their own thoughts to notice faults in me.

I have a healthy degree of humility:

"For everyone who exalts himself will be humbled, and he who humbles himself will be exalted." Luke 14:11 (ESV)

And I have a healthy sense of belonging:

"But to all who did receive him, who believed in his name, he gave the right to become children of God." John 1:12 (ESV)

More importantly, I understand that my life isn't about me anymore. It's for Jesus.

"I have been crucified with Christ; and it is no longer I who live, but Christ lives in me; and the life which I now live in the flesh I live by faith in the Son of God, who loved me and gave Himself up for me." Galatians 2:20 (NASB)

Hope
BY HEIDI RENEE

Hope is not a word that is used often enough in our world of constant chaos. The idea of hope is mostly expressed as airy packages of well wishes often said when there are no other words available. I do not know what to say, therefore I will be generic. Hope seems to be an afterthought or a last resort in times of crisis. I often wonder how we arrived at this place of lacking something so vital.

Hope is not the first emotion that flickers when our hearts are in the dark. No. Too often we fall on fear, doubt, despair, and hopelessness. Why do we do this to ourselves?

A few years ago, I wrote a book about my family's journey through adoption and the first several years after our son arrived home. While writing, a quote from a Robert Frost poem echoed in my head and often woke me from a sound sleep.

Two roads diverged in a wood, and I—
I took the one less traveled by,
And that has made all the difference.
I envisioned my husband and I standing at a fork in the road. We were on a road that we had never been on, didn't ask to be on, didn't want to be on, and didn't understand.

We had waited in tremendous anticipation for our son to come home. Every day, I held on to the hope we would again receive pictures of his sweet face and hear something positive about our case. Adoptions in Guatemala were slowing and the political climate surrounding international adoption was beyond tense. Still, we leaned into the hope that he would be home sooner rather than later. That day finally came a few weeks after a visit for his first birthday.

When our son was placed in my arms, I knew something was amiss. Hope turned to worry and panic in a split second. As we stepped off the plane, we rushed up the jet bridge and drove straight to the hospital. Over the next few months we watched our world crumble as diagnosis after diagnosis was made and on the same day my father lost his battle with cancer, my son was diagnosed with cerebral palsy. Crushed is the only word that I am able to muster, even now after so many years, to describe that period in my life.

I did not possess a deep faith in Christ when we adopted our son. Church was not a place of solace for us during this period in our lives. In fact, I did everything I could to run from God and the church. Sympathy was a curse. Every kind comment felt like a thorn pricking an open wound. One of the most joyous moments in our lives was being met with "I'm sorry."; "That's awful!" and "You should sue!" Our days consisted of countless appointments and a constant barrage of therapists and educators in our home. Hope was simply not in my vocabulary.

While researching this idea of hope, I stumbled upon an archaic definition of the word. In that context, hope is described as a feeling of trust. I find God's brilliance in marrying the two ideas of hope and trust. What I experienced with our son trashed my ability to trust. I was fearful of others intentions toward our family, especially my son. I remained silent for many years, focusing on providing our son with everything that he needed. In quietness I moved forward. As a release, I wrote about our journey and kept my head in the game for my son. A medical professional had told us that our son would not have survived another month in Guatemala. My son's second chance at life gave me tremendous focus and purpose.

In quietness and trust is your strength.
–Isaiah 30:15 NIV

As the years passed, our son overcame the low expectations of those early dark days. He showed us a zeal and joy for life that continuously spills over each and every single person he meets. I felt a gentle pull from God asking us to trust Him and become part of a church again. It was terrifying, but we did it anyway. We began to not only learn but also trust His purpose in giving us our son. My heart slowly softened and I began to trust others again. What's more, our son's achievements began building hope.

No one was more surprised than I was when the call to adopt again fell on my heart. While we had originally planned to welcome a second child shortly after our son arrived, we had made peace with the idea that our family was complete. Someone once told me we make plans and God laughs. Low and behold, here we were in our social worker's office discussing another international adoption. A few weeks later, I received a phone call about a little girl in Bulgaria. This child was blind in one eye and had unknown vision in the other. She needed a forever family fast or her file would go to the bottom of the pile.

We had less than a week to decide whether we would accept the referral or not. I remember sobbing on my bed, asking God for direction. Our hearts had said yes from the moment we learned about her, but hope and trust were overcome by fear, doubt, and worry. Uncertainty swallowed me whole. The phone rang. It was the agency. They needed an answer. We said Yes!

We began her adoption process with a deep faith and trust that God was in control. There were countless variables completely out of our control. Would we be able to provide for both children's needs? Would our application be accepted given our son's needs and my husbands newly diagnosed chronic illness? Despite all of these questions, I still felt hope. Hope for our daughter's future. Hope for our family's future.

My heart had done a complete 180-degree turn. The next eighteen months brought pure hope. Our adoption began with zero funding, but was fully funded by the end of the process. We prayerfully asked family and friends for help and trusted their intentions toward our family. We held onto hope that this process would proceed smoothly and banked on God being with us at every step, whether forward or backward.

Hope became tangible. It was in family and friends dropping off items for our rummage sale, attending our fundraiser, and releasing balloons to celebrate our little girl's birthday while we were still waiting. Our daughter arrived to a sea of support and love. Our family of four would not exist had we not leaned on hope and trusted in Christ. Hope has a different meaning to me after completing our family.

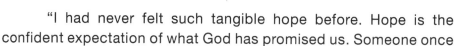

"I had never felt such tangible hope before. Hope is the confident expectation of what God has promised us. Someone once told me we make plans and God laughs."

I believe we hold hope to a high level of expectation different than what Christ holds for us. We hope that a certain thing will (or will not) happen. The world's definition of hope is often a wish. We must remember our God is not a genie. Our God does not grant wishes. He does nothing by chance.

"But now, Lord, what do I look for? My hope is in you."
Psalm 39:7 NIV

What if we allowed hope to be open-ended? What if we purposely placed hope in Christ as our default setting? What if we are willing to say, 'I am enough in Christ and will trust in Him who is the ultimate Hope'?

Hope is readily available and waiting for us every second of every day.

I am enough in Christ to hold hope in Him and his promises. Every second of every day.

Joyful

BY STEPHANIE MILLER

"The joy of the lord is my strength."
(Nehemiah 8:10 New International Version)

When we look to the comforts of this world to fill a God-shaped void, we encounter a problem; we end up searching for contentment in all the wrong places. Before I surrendered my life to Christ, I chased fleeting moments of happiness by the ways of this world, in an effort to erase the emptiness I felt. I sought satisfaction from men, craving the attention and love I never received from my alcoholic father. My life was a series of disastrous relationships, detrimental habits, and dangerous partying.

Even after I confessed to Jesus Christ as my Lord and Savior, my heart wasn't fully transformed. I still looked for things to make me happy. Experiencing moments of bliss was the same as being happy in my eyes, but God graciously showed me the difference through a stormy season. Looking back now, I had to have a breakdown before a breakthrough -- that is, before I could appreciate the joy that abiding in the Lord brings. True joy, as I discovered, is only found in a deep and intimate relationship with God.

I met my now husband in the fall of 2010, and we were married in the spring of 2014. As a new wife-- a new Army wife -- I walked away from my career as a teacher and followed my husband to a different state which we would call home for the next four years. It was during the first year of our marriage that I experienced a loneliness and depression like I had never known before. My husband worked every day and often well into the night. The silence was suffocating. Not only did I not leave the house, but I also didn't even leave my bed. Brushing my teeth and taking a shower had become overwhelming chores that I seldom had enough energy to carry out. I knew my depression wasn't only affecting me, but also my marriage, as well. My husband didn't know what to do; I didn't even know what to do. I felt like I was in a fog, not living but just existing. One night, after I had been crying for several hours, I grabbed my Bible on a whim. From a point of desperation and despair, I cried out to God to show me my purpose. As I flipped open my Bible, it landed on Jerimiah 29:11.

"For I know the plans I have for you," declares the Lord, "plans to prosper you and not to harm you, plans to give you hope and a future."

That was all I needed. Confirmation that I wasn't wasting my life, and that if I would commit my life to Him, He would show me the way. I started to read more of my Bible and surround myself with Christian women who listened without judgment as I shared about my struggle with depression. In the safety of a loving and supporting community, God slowly moved the rock I had been living under and held my hand as I climbed out. It wasn't just a day-by-day decision to choose Him, but moment-by-moment. At first it took an exorbitant amount of effort to find activities and experiences that I enjoyed, but as I grew in my relationship with God, it became easier to see God's blessings all around me.

God exhibited His goodness and faithfulness by rescuing me from that debilitating depression. Recognizing and appreciating His love is where my joy comes from. The more I depend on Him, the more He reveals his gracious nature to me. I am joyful in the Lord because He lives in me. Apart from my relationship with Him, I wouldn't know what joy is. I would still be looking to the comforts of this world for happiness. True joy in the Lord isn't a feeling, but a choice, and choosing joy gives us the strength we need in every season.

"We have this hope as an anchor for the soul, firm and secure."
Hebrews 6:19

His strength is enough to withstand even the strongest storm. I'm no longer riding the roller coaster of emotion, experiencing every high and low by letting my emotions dictate my behavior, but I am fully anchored in hope because of my joy in Christ.

Does this mean that I have a permanent smile plastered on my face? Does this mean I turn a blind eye to what's going on around me? No. It is not perfect; it is quite messy and hard. It is challenging to look for the good in an extremely painful situation.

That's the thing, though. Having hope and being joyful isn't about constructing a false façade that hides deep pain. It is about looking to God-given blessings even during difficult times. Being joyful in the middle of a storm is not easy, nor is it automatic. It requires us to make a conscious choice to dwell on our current circumstances or direct our minds and hearts to the one who is "greater than the one who is in the world."

"You, dear children, are from God and have overcome them, because the one who is in you is greater than the one who is in the world." 1 John 4:4

Intuitively, I understand this verse, but overcoming the spirit of the antichrist has been especially exhausting lately.

It was a Saturday afternoon several months ago when I found out my father had fallen into his addiction again after some time in recovery. I was on the phone with my mother, and as she was talking, I sensed that something wasn't quite right. She had been spending most of her days and nights away from the house, so without thinking, I blurted out the question:

"Is Dad drinking again?"

"Yes," she replied.

My heart sank. A million emotions erupted inside of me. I was angry at him for throwing away his newly sober life. I was hurt that he once again chose drugs and alcohol over his family. I was confused as to why he went back to the chains of addiction after being set free. I felt like a mean trick had been played on me. It was as if I had been given a taste of what a relationship with my dad could be like, then to just have it ripped out of my hands.

As the details of this episode emerged, it became clear that it was more than just a slip, but a premeditated act. He had carefully crafted a story that convinced a new doctor to prescribe medication that no addict should handle without the involvement of his support network. Once he manipulated the doctor into prescribing him these drugs, it wasn't long before he also started drinking again.

In church, on the day after I received the news about my dad, I experienced something that I never thought possible. They played all of my favorite worship songs including, "Good, Good Father," but I couldn't utter a single word. It took all that I had not to break down into tears that morning. I started to question if God even cared about me and my family.

"How can God be good if He allowed this to happen?"

I struggled to reconcile how I felt about what was happening with my knowledge of who God is. I played Hillary Scott's "Thy will," Mercy Me's "Even if," and Tenth Avenue North's "Worn" on repeat. I slowly started to come to terms with my new reality. The sober dad I had seen only a few months before may never be again. As I thought back to our last visit, I felt guilty for not having appreciated his sobriety more. I grieved the death of the relationship I thought I was going to have with him, and the death of the relationship I thought my future children would have with him. In that first month after finding out about my dad's relapse, I fought hard against the depression that loomed over me and tried to find something to be thankful for. Joy was non-existent to me as I questioned God's goodness and faithfulness. I could feel all of my hope and faith in God start to slowly slip away as He remained silent when I cried out to Him for answers.

Then, the next month, we received news that hit me like a lightning bolt.

I was pregnant.

This was a complete surprise to my husband and I, who had only just started talking about starting a family. After the initial shock and excitement wore off, I felt joy, but also a deep sadness.

Yes, I was growing a tiny little miracle inside of me, but I felt like I didn't deserve this baby -- not with everything that was going on in my own family. To make it even more complicated, I also had two very close friends who were struggling with infertility and telling them I was pregnant seemed almost cruel. I was heartbroken for my friends; I was sure God had made a mistake and I had somehow stolen their blessing.

The enemy did everything in his power to steal, kill, and destroy any joy over my pregnancy during the first few months. I told myself repeatedly that something was going to happen and to not get too attached to this life growing inside of me. I was scared to let myself be joyful over my pregnancy, afraid that it would be taken away from me, just like the relationship with my father had been.

Then one morning after talking to a trusted friend about all of my worries and insecurities, I made a decision to allow myself to feel the pure joy that God was bringing into my life.

"Consider it pure joy, my brothers and sisters, whenever you face trials of many kinds, because you know that the testing of your faith produces perseverance. Let perseverance finish its work so that you may be mature and complete, not lacking anything."

- James 1:2-4

Notice how this verse says "consider" and not that you will "automatically assume." Consider means to think carefully about something. Often our initial response to trials of many kinds is anything but joy, and we have to work to look beyond our circumstances to God within us.

God placed an outward blessing on my family to remind me of His goodness and faithfulness.

Having my daughter, even in the center of what is going on with my father, has been a bigger blessing than I even could have imagined.

She does so many things that make me smile and laugh. She isn't responsible for my joy, of course, but I recognize that the loving and caring nature of God to give me this precious girl is where my joy comes from. I affectionately call her my "Sunshine in the Storm."

My little sunshine is too young to be aware of the storm that surrounds her. She will not know her grandpa to be any way other than what he is now. However, when I look at my father, I see God's love for him and his potential in Christ. I see the father, husband, son, and grandpa he is meant to be. I recall an earlier time when healing sat on the throne of his heart. But what I really long for, what keeps me up at night and praying on my knees, is for Jesus to occupy his heart.

Sadness.

I see my daughter, who sits on his lap only a few seconds before she giggles and squirms. I see a smile come across my father's face, in response to her childlike innocence.

Joy.

I watch my father interact with my daughter, a shell of a man with momentary glimmers of hope in his eyes. Tears of sadness and joy stream down my face. I consciously smile through these tears and reach for my squirmy little girl.

*"Just like a hundred-dollar bill found on the ground,
no matter how bruised and torn, or what I've been through,
to Him, I will never lose my value."*

I am Loved

BY DEBORAH WARREN

"Love is patient, love is kind. It does not envy, it does not boast, it is not proud. It does not dishonor others, it is not self-seeking, it is not easily angered, it keeps no record of wrongs. Love does not delight in evil but rejoices with the truth. It always protects, always trusts, always hopes, always perseveres." (1 Corinthians 13:4-7 New International Version)

Before I came to know Jesus as my "all that", I thought I'd been born into the Twilight Zone. I was sure the people I lived with, who said they were my family, were really aliens from another planet. Satan seemed to be working through them to persuade me that love was pretty much the opposite of the way it's described in 1 Corinthians 13.

My life began with rejection. Even in the womb, I heard senseless sounds that made me want to stay inside. And when I did finally come out, it was with a scowl on my face and a bad attitude in my heart. No, the love I received from my family was not patient or kind. They didn't protect me, trust me, or instill hope and perseverance.

In the early years, being loved by my parents meant being disappointed repeatedly. It meant hearing that you were "laid by a buzzard and hatched by the sun" over and over, and that your gums were poisonous like a snake and would kill anyone if you bit them. It seemed that from birth, I already had three strikes against me I had no power to change: my skin was too dark, my lips were too big, and my gums were too purple. I was most certainly not the favorite child. What they did for my siblings, they didn't do for me. Being loved was something I deeply desired. My love tank was as dry as the Sahara Desert, and I had no idea how to fill it up.

Everybody on this earth craves and needs to be loved. Even though we're different on the outside: the color of our skin, hair and eyes, the texture of our hair, our shapes, our genders, our height or our weight; we all share something on the inside. We need to be loved. We all desire it with nearly every waking breath. We all look to find that special someone to love us and who we can love back. It makes sense given that God is Love, and from the moment our souls leave heaven, we want and long for the day we return to Him, and to His love. Even though we're born not really knowing what love is, there is something deep down in us that just knows that love is supposed to make us feel good, not bad. Love is supposed to put a force field around us to keep us from the hurt, pain, and loneliness this world cranks out. It's not supposed to lie or disappoint or speak badly. But that was my love training from the day I came out of the womb.

In those early years, because of how my family treated me, I made up little stories that my dad must have had me through an affair and my "real" mother had died in childbirth with me. I told myself the woman passing herself off as my mom must have been forced to care for me since I no longer had a mother of my own. This was the only explanation that made sense to my young mind because I couldn't possibly fathom how a real mother could treat her own child the way she treated me. It was a question I posed to myself almost daily. My mom and dad seemed to only expect bad from me and nothing good. I was always blamed for every wicked thing that happened in the house, but, after I turned seven, things began to change.

My life got really interesting when I turned seven. I got

baptized and had a crazy good baptism experience. I approached my baptism literally kicking and screaming like someone possessed, but, when I was dunked in the water, I saw a vision of Jesus in the water with me. Peace fell over every part of me, and the kicking and screaming turned to laughter and tears of joy! My love tank began to fill up and the empty places weren't so empty anymore. Something phenomenal had just happened, but I had no idea what it was. In the days and weeks that followed, I continued to question the situation with my parents. Then, one day, through the tears, a voice spoke back, and everything began to make sense. That was my first personal encounter with God, and suddenly, I came out of the fog. He gave me answers to my questions and joy filled my heart for the first time in my life. I finally felt there was somebody there for me and I ran to Him as often as I could to learn how to deal with all the bad stuff happening around me. I grew calmer as I talked to God more. I felt hope begin to rise in me at the possibility for good things to come as His voice repeatedly instructed me to hold on and trust Him. That's what kept me going until the day my dad changed his relationship with me.

One Saturday evening about a year after my baptism, my dad went to the cabinet to get a glass and discovered one of them was broken. As usual, I was blamed, and in his anger, he took out his belt to spank me – No questions asked. I was little, but I was mad as heck! Here again, I was blamed for doing something I hadn't done. Why, I wondered for the millionth time, was I going through this? Out of fear and frustration, something in me popped and I shouted, 'I didn't do it! It was Wanda!'

Silence.

Slowly, my dad's eyes seemed to see the truth. His ears heard it, too.

He asked my sister directly if I was telling the truth and she finally confessed. He left the kitchen, went to his room and said nothing else. I can only imagine that Jesus was doing something way down deep inside him because that was the last spanking I ever received from my dad and it was after this day I started being a "daddy's girl."

I started hanging out more with my earthly dad, experiencing a love I'd never experienced before (and still didn't' receive from my mom). I talked to my dad constantly about anything he was working on around the house and he taught me so many things about fixing cars, repairing the house, reading maps, and so much more. Anything I asked about, he taught me. My love tank was filling up more, and I got closer and closer to my earthly dad and closer to my heavenly dad.

Unfortunately, rejection was the same old song playing over and over with my mom. She still spewed out negativity about my skin color, trying to make me believe that anyone who had a dark complexion, like me, was dumb, stupid and ugly. God stayed by my side, though, providing what I came to call a "play mom" in every city where I lived since leaving home, to give me the motherly love I'd never received. These women embraced, loved and encouraged me and made me feel I was all that and a bag of chips. Because of them, I was strong enough to face my mom once each year for a three-day visit.

At 25, I was starting over after another horrible break-up where rejection had once again won out. I had just moved to Greensboro, NC, where I landed a well-paying job, a terrific church, and my fourth "play mom". A year later, my mom announced she was coming for a 5-day visit. I immediately went to God in a panic because of the length of the visit.

How in the world would I handle having her there for five days, I asked Him?

He calmly told me to trust Him to handle it.

Her first day there, she asked to speak to me alone. While sitting on my bed, getting almost sick imagining what would come out of her mouth, she told me what I'd never expected to hear in a million years! She explained that from watching a segment of the Oprah Winfrey Show about having a favorite child, she realized she'd treated me different from my siblings. She wanted to say that she was sorry.

Wow! I knew I liked Oprah for some reason!

On that day, God used Oprah as an instrument of care and concern for children like me. Through her, God had done what He'd promised! It was handled! God was true and real, and He could be trusted! That would mark the beginning of the end of my rejection and the deepening of my love and faith in God.

After Jesus "took the wheel", the sense of rejection was finally relieved, and I learned what it really meant to be loved God's way. My smile began to shine...purple gums and all. In the years that followed my mom's revelation, she and I grew closer. I give all praise to the power of the Holy Spirit in leading and empowering me to stay willing to accept my mother's love, even after years of deliberate mistreatment. He gave me eyes to finally see why she'd hurt me. I learned that hurt people, hurt people, and that the root of all negativity is hurt.

Incredibly, at 46, the day came when my mom said I was one of the best things that had ever happened to her. I knew then that my God was faithful and would do what He promised; He would love All of Me!

Jesus is still working on the scar tissue of rejection inside me and re-teaching me what unconditional love is, but there is no doubt that I am loved beyond measure. He continually shows me in so many ways. Absolutely, being loved from the beginning would have been easier, but that rejection by my 'alien' family led me to have the close, loving relationship I now have with Him. I doubt I'd know Him as father, friend, husband, healer, provider, or protector without that experience. As surely as we have God, we have love. Look again to see it, or, give it to Him and He will create it. Just trust and be loved.

"And so we know and rely on the love God has for us.
God is love. Whoever lives in love lives in God, and God in them."
1 John 4:16 | NIV

Finding Peace in a Stressful World

BY CHOU HALLEGRA

In this world full of hurt, injustice, greed, and chaos, peace seems like an illusion. People chase after the next thing, person, activity, or occasion that, they believe, will give them peace. We've all heard, "when things settle down, I will..." or "as soon as my kids, my spouse, my work..., I will..."

I have been falling into that trap for as long I can remember. However, as soon as the next thing, person, activity, or occasion came, something else happened and I found myself sacrificing gratitude, contentment and peace until a new deadline or circumstance came and went. Peace seemed to be unattainable, a never-ending merry go-round on which my horse would never cross the finish line.

This is where I was just a little over a year ago, wondering, amid the chaos, where is the peace that we are promised in the Bible?

Something had to give.

It feels like it was just yesterday that I was inside a helicopter, laying on a stretcher. I was being airlifted to a hospital, unable to speak or move the left side of my body. What's going on? How long will this last? Will I ever speak again? What will happen to my kids?

I felt powerless. There was nothing I could do to change

the situation. The medical staff assured me that they were doing everything they knew to do, but I needed more.

I like to figure things out. I like to make things happen. I'm known as the connector, the case manager, the resource coordinator. I'm a mover and a shaker, yet I couldn't move anything at all in that moment.

Once at the hospital, I was sent to the Intensive Care Unit and placed on stroke protocol. Everyone was baffled; this couldn't be happening, I was only 33 years old and I had no issues with cholesterol, blood pressure or my heart. Yet, this was happening and no one knew what the future would hold.

Then, out of the blue, a sense of peace washed over me like a gently flowing river. In this seemingly hopeless situation, I accepted my powerlessness over people, things, and situations. I accepted that my peace is found in Christ and Christ alone. In that moment, John 14:27 made perfect sense: "Peace I leave with you; my peace I give you. I do not give to you as the world gives. Do not let your hearts be troubled and do not be afraid."

Lasting peace was not to be found in the doctors who were treating me. Peace would not come from knowing whether I would talk or walk again. Peace was not to be found in figuring out what might happen to my kids. Peace is not found on this earth nor in the things and people in it. Peace is found in Christ alone.

At the time I'm writing this, it's been about 18-months since that day in the helicopter. I spent almost a month in medical facilities, followed by intense therapy at home and in outpatient clinics. Today, I am able to speak almost as clearly as before, but once in a while, I still find myself searching for words or saying something out of context. I can walk but I still struggle with balance issues which require me to use a walker.

I have come such a long way but nerve pain and physical

limitations remind me of where I have been. In many ways, I am not the same woman physically, mentally, and spiritually. My perspective on life and suffering has changed and my faith grew immensely. God has the power to eliminate all the consequences of this experience, but as of today, He continues to use it to bring me and many others closer to Him. I consider myself healed because I no longer put peace on hold. I no longer wait for that thing, person, activity, or occasion to bring me contentment. I am alive and doing more for God than I ever did before.

During my time of physical, mental, and spiritual healing, I have come to understand a few things about finding peace in a stressful world:

1. "Jesus Christ is the same yesterday and today and forever" Hebrews 13:8

Jesus, who is not just the son of God but God incarnate, does not change like the weather or the clothes we wear. He does not change as our emotions change. He does not even change as our circumstances change. He does not change when everyone around you has changed.

I need you to grasp this: Because Jesus will never change we can trust Him with our ever-changing lives. We can trust Him when we are facing uncertain times. We can trust Him with our children, our marriages, our careers, our lives.

We can trust Him because He never fails and He will carry us through, just as He has already done so many times before. When life gets overwhelming, hold on to His faithfulness and remember Psalm 46:1, "God is our refuge and strength, an ever-present help in times of need."

2. Peace is a state of mind

One of the main reasons we fail to accept peace through Christ is that we expect people and things to provide the peace we need, which is impossible. Even if your kids did everything you ever told them, something else will go wrong. Even if your husband listened to everything you say, something else will bring tension. Even if you had the perfect job, the perfect car, the perfect church, something else will shake you. It might be traffic, violence in our world, your health or maybe the death of a loved one.

Our life on earth is full of unexpected stressors and things that are totally out of our control. These situations leave us feeling powerless, but when you realize that peace is a state of mind, you will never be hopeless. This is why Romans 12:2 tells us to not conform to this world, "but be transformed by the renewing of our minds." When you renew your mind, you can be peaceful when your bank account is in the negative. You can be peaceful after a job loss. You can be peaceful when you are faced with difficulties of any kind. It all depends on what thoughts you entertain in your mind.

Psalm 23:7 tells us we become what we think. When faced with difficulties, do you tell yourself "I can't do this" or "this is the end of me"? These types of statements will only increase your unease. In other words, you are speaking chaos into the situation. Remember, there is power of life and death at the tip of our tongues (Proverbs 18:21). Start speaking peace into your life and you will start feeling peaceful.

When you receive an unexpected medical diagnosis, remind yourself that God is your Healer (Exodus 15:26). This might not make your condition go away, but the angst and fear that comes with such things will no longer paralyze you because God heals however, He thinks is best.

When bills are piling up and you're not sure how you will make ends meet, tell yourself "The Lord is my provider". The bills might still be there past their due dates, God might be giving you the opportunity to exercise your faith muscles. Eventually, He will take care of it somehow and in His timing. He might provide extra hours at work or a new client or contract for your business, which will bring in additional income. He might even send an angel to pay a bill or two for you or He might touch the hearts of those you owe and make them kind enough to extend your grace period, not charge you interest, or even cancel the debt altogether. I have seen God do all these things in my life or in the lives of others. He can do it for you as well because He hasn't changed.

"Peace is a state of mind. You can bring peace to any situation you find yourself in when you make a conscious effort to focus your mind on God and not on the situation itself."

You should still take actions when needed, but your mind starts seeing God working it out and anxiety no longer controls your life. Didn't Jesus say, "Don't let your heart be troubled, trust in God and trust in me?" (John 14:1). The more we trust in God, the more at peace we will feel.

3. You are not God

This should be obvious, right? And yet, are we not 'playing God' when trying to fix, manage, and control people and situations? Many times, we end up doing this unintentionally. Perhaps you are going through something and you can't wait for it to be over. You prayed. You fasted. You talked to mentors and counselors. And these circumstances won't change! In most cases, this is when we try to manipulate the situation, to take charge and get it over with. Does any of this sound familiar?

We create more chaos and stress by trying to handle our problems on our own, instead of letting God take care of it. We want things done our way and on our timing. Doesn't that defeat the purpose of praying? Remember, it is written, "For my thoughts are not your thoughts, neither are your ways my ways" declares the Lord" (Isaiah 55:8). Then why do we even try to have it our way? Why carry everything to the Lord in prayer and then pick it up again? Isn't God strong enough to handle it? Isn't He wise enough to figure it out? God is bigger, stronger, and smarter than all of us. We need to stop leaning on our own understanding and instead acknowledge Him in all our ways so He can make our paths straight (Proverbs 3:6).

We tend to mess things up even more when we play God. Remember when Sarah was so worried about not having a child that she couldn't wait for God's promise to be manifested? She got restless and took matters in her own hands, telling her husband to have a child with her servant. She thought that would fix things, a quick and simple remedy. Everything went wrong for Sarah. She and her husband had the servant's child, but still, there was no peace to be found. Sarah became jealous of the servant and began to mistreat her. She thought she had fixed her problem but now she wasn't at peace with the solution she came up with on her own. (You can read about this story in Genesis 16)

If we're honest, we can all relate to Sarah. We all tend to hurry things a bit, or manipulate situations just enough to have our way. We don't realize that by doing so, we are telling God that we know better. Nobody would ever want to make such a statement but our actions send this message loud and clear. When we act in this manner, we make a big mess in our lives and the lives of others.

Next time you want to take matters into your own hands, remind yourself – He is God and I am not. This will lessen the need to manipulate your circumstances or control their outcomes. It also helps to "cast your cares on the One who cares for you".
(1 Peter 5:7).

In closing, when life gets tough and stressors steal away your joy, first remember that God is still on the throne, He hasn't changed and you can still trust Him. Then, change your focus from your trouble to God's faithfulness. Finally, relinquish the need to be in control. Let God be God and all will be well.

I Am Positive Through God's Faithfulness

BY SHAWNEE PENKACIK

"For I know the plans I have for you," declares the Lord, "plans to prosper you and not to harm you, plans to give you hope and a future." - Jeremiah 29:11

Graduating from high school is a major milestone for a young person. For me, it was an awesome accomplishment because the circumstances of my young life made the odds of it ever happening very slim.

Abuse issues at home and bullying at school necessitated a fresh start before my adult life even began.

At age 18, thanks to a caring cousin, I moved to a new city with a much bigger school. While the change was needed, it wasn't easy. This was very scary! I had grown up in small town America where everyone knew everyone and most folks didn't lock their doors at night. This was not the case in my new home.

When I arrived at my new school, I remember shyly asking the guidance counselor if it was even possible for me to finish high school on time. She assured me that it was and gave me my new schedule and a plan. I used that plan to become more disciplined.

I spent long nights in my books, studying hard, and finally made it to graduation day. My family and friends were impressed that I did what was said to be impossible. My cousin was thrilled and threw a party that included our extended family and people from church who were near and dear to my heart. One of those was my mentor and friend.

My mentor was someone I looked up to for very good reasons. First, she loved the Lord wholeheartedly and this was evident in how she talked, how she treated others, and how she loved her family. Her speech reflected that of the fruits of the spirit – She didn't speak an unkind word to anyone. Second, she served others. She sang in church, as well as the community, in choir and in duets with her husband. To me, she resembled the Proverbs 31 wife and mom – a Woman of Valor. I remember feeling honored that she (and her husband) had taken the time to encourage me, believe in me, and love me like I was her own daughter.

As it turned out, my mentor couldn't make it to the graduation party, but when we met at some point beforehand, she blessed me with some amazing gifts: A bag of potpourri for my room, a beautiful figurine from a collection I had only dreamed of owning, and tons of scripture to remind me of God's promises for my life. After saying a number of thank yous, giving hugs, and being in awe of my blessings, I noticed a line of scripture on the bag of potpourri. My eyes welled up with tears as I read Jeremiah 29:11. Put simply, that verse assures me, 'God has a great plan for your life, Shawnee.' This promise of HOPE and a FUTURE leads to why I am positive.

Don't get me wrong, it's hard to stay positive in a world that seems to have adopted an attitude of negativity. Social media is littered with pessimism and resentment. Family, friends, acquaintances and celebrities belittle each other, posting worries instead of gratitude. On the television screen, we see fires, terror attacks, shootings, and neighbors being downright rude to one another. Especially troubling, our children, who should be living lives that are care-free, are bullied and burdened by these forces that contribute to a world of complaining and loss.

But when we focus on the negative things, we tend to become depressed because we are thinking about what we lack, instead of celebrating what God has blessed us.

I often say that God does not want us to live a life that is broken, busted, and disgusted. He wants us to live a life full of joy, hope, and love.

So, let's take a look at what being positive looks like. First, being positive is about trusting the Lord in every aspect for your life. Now, that is easier said than done. I can write that you need to trust the Lord but yes, I know that actually doing it isn't always easy, so don't beat yourself up if you find yourself struggling with negativity. After all, it's inevitable that we, as human beings, will encounter internal and external challenges.

Personally, I forgot about God's promise of Hope and a Future, when my son Jackson was diagnosed with a rare genetic disease that I had never even heard of. Worry and doubt clouded my mind. I struggled to remain positive when my husband lost his job just six months after moving to a new city. We believed it was God's will for us to move to Phoenix, but then suddenly things fell apart.

Is it easy to remain positive when your own health declines and walking becomes a struggle at only 40 years of age? The answer is a resounding "NO". But, as in all things, the Bible can bring comfort in these times.

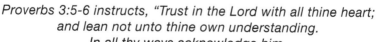

Proverbs 3:5-6 instructs, "Trust in the Lord with all thine heart;
and lean not unto thine own understanding.
In all thy ways acknowledge him,
and he shall direct thy paths."

In John 16, Jesus foresees the day when He will no longer

walk among His disciples, explaining to them that, through Him, their grief will turn to joy. In verse 33, He says, "I have told you all this so that you may have peace in me. Here on earth you will have many trials and sorrows. But take heart, because I have overcome the world." In this world, we will face difficult times. This is because our world is broken…It's a world in need of Jesus. But during those storms, we can remain positive remembering that God has been faithful.

As flawed human beings, this doesn't necessarily come naturally. When my son Jackson was not waking up to eat, wasn't doing what he was naturally supposed to do, I remember sitting at his hospital bed and crying out, "Lord, I know you do miracles so I need one NOW. Please give me wisdom in what to do for Jackson. Please don't let him die."

A whole new world of shots, biopsies, feeding tubes, and even brain surgery entered our lives. I'm overjoyed to say that today, Jackson is a happy twelve-year-old boy who still lives with the illness but faces it with inspiring courage. God was, and remains, faithful.

To remind me of the positive things in my life, I keep a journal. It's filled with short entries where I write down a few things that happened that day and count my blessings. I love pulling it out when I am struggling because it reminds me how God has carried me, how much He loves me, and how He is continually faithful. This is how I trust the Lord in every aspect of my life.

Another exercise that helps me look on the bright side, is my blessings jar. Grab any jar, a spaghetti sauce jar for example, and if you're crafty, maybe decorate it with ribbon, buttons, and charms. Commit to writing three blessings on a slip of paper every day and drop it in the jar. Simple things, but things that remind you of your blessings instead of your worries. So one day, the blessings at the forefront of my mind were my coffee, my Bible, and my bed. Over time, you will be amazed at how your mindset begins to change. You start to look on the positive side rather than the gloomy one. You appreciate simple things like a cup of coffee. Being positive is a mindset. It's compelling your mind to be set on the good things in life.

When I was a child, I attended a program called the Missionettes. They had us memorize a lot of scripture.

One verse that is the cornerstone of the program is Philippians 4:8: "Finally, brethren, whatsoever things are true, whatsoever things are honest, whatsoever things are just, whatsoever things are pure, whatsoever things are lovely, whatsoever things are of good report; if there be any virtue, and if there be any praise, think on these things." So what does this mean?

What do I know to be true? Well, I know God loves me. We find evidence of this in John 3:16.

What do I know to be honest? I know God is honest and that He has a plan for my life.

What do I know to be just? I know God's commandments and purpose are fair.

What do I know is pure? I know God's promises, as found in His word, are pure.

What do I know is lovely? Lovely, to me, is the fact that I am God's child. I am chosen.

What do I know is of good report? I know I have good qualities that God has given me.

Think on the things that build you up not the things, situations, or people that tear you down.

Remember, even as we cultivate a positive outlook, life will still be life. Bad things happen. We live in a fallen world. Just because you are a Christian doesn't mean you will be exempt from life's challenges. Far from it. We may struggle even more when doing what God has called us to do because we are most likely making the enemy mad. There is nothing the devil likes more than a fallen world filled with discord and disunity. After all, he is the author of confusion.

What makes the difference for the Faithful is walking through the storm and placing it into the hands of the Master saying, "God, I trust you. Lord, I know you have my finances, my health, my family, and my job. They are all in your hands. I know Lord, you work all things together for the good of those who love you and are called according to your purpose. Thank you Lord for working this out. Give me wisdom. Help me to do what is right and honorable to you. Thank you, Jesus. Amen."

Do you remember the story in the Bible where Jesus was asleep on the boat? The disciples lost all hope and faith in a future. During these times, we are called on to remember when God has been faithful to us and know that He will do it again. God is the same yesterday, today, and forever, just as it is written in Hebrews 13:8. He never changes and never fails.

Being positive isn't easy. You will fall from time to time. But, just like regular exercise, as you do it more, you will get your mind trained to think on the blessings of life even in the midst of struggles. Eventually, you will emerge from feelings of negativity more quickly and better understand God's plans to give you hope and a future.

You are Powerful
How to Rise up to
your True Potential
BY EMMA SCHILTER

Power gets a bad rap sometimes. Being powerful can come across as negative and aggressive – Leaders of huge companies that state legal battles are powerful. Dictators are powerful. 'No,' we tell

ourselves, 'I can't claim that I am powerful! That'd be egotistical, prideful, and greedy.' But what if I told you that it's possible to understand and live out our "power" while also being humble, loving and kind?

The thing is, I totally understand why you'd think that unleashing your power is scary. Being Christian women, we need to respect and submit to our husbands, care for our children, and always give ourselves to everyone around us. We are to be selfless and care for everyone. You know what I'm talking about ladies... We have to become "Wonder Woman"! If we were to ever unleash our power, we fear that the people around us will feel smaller or of lesser value which, of course, isn't true.

What the world doesn't exactly realize is that, without us needing to say or act upon anything - wives, mothers, sisters, daughters, and girlfriends are the most powerful beings on this planet. We are truly capable of anything we set our minds to - I mean we LITERALLY birth every human that is on this planet. God gave us this incredible and miraculous ability to grow a complex and amazing human inside of us. It's a beautiful and inspiring thing!

We are all unique individuals and we have a purpose on this planet. We are made in the image of God and we are filled with the Holy Spirit - THE MOST POWERFUL force in the entire universe. God is in us, which makes us unstoppable.

But here's the problem: We constantly belittle our true potential (a gift from God) because we are fearful of how others will view us, think of us, or react to us. We are afraid to show our true selves and are fearful that by doing so, it would make us less of a woman, mom, wife, or girlfriend. WHY do we do this? Why do we hide behind the expectations of our family and friends instead of elevating ourselves and our gifts that God has blessed us with? Why do we have this never-ending narrative in our minds that we are "less than"...That we are not capable, qualified, or good enough?

Listen up! And listen good...You ARE enough. You are capable. You are qualified. You are talented. You have the Holy Spirit in you, and you have been called for something. God has literally engrossed His own power within you to use for His plan and His purpose. If you do not allow yourself to utilize this wonderful gift that is POWER, you are doing a disservice to yourself and those around you.

If you feel like something is missing, it probably is. You can run away from it, hide from it and scream really, really loud at it, but if something is pounding on your heart you may want to start listening and opening your heart and your mind. You might not know it, but just by leaning into God's power and plan, you will affect many lives around you - just by being, YOU. I learned this after I kept running away from God. He put something on my heart, and I wanted nothing to do with it. I kept telling myself that I was absolutely not capable or even worthy of such a venture. I STILL struggle with this internal narrative [voice in my head], but I've also learned how to overcome it.

You guys, I'll be honest with you, I'm only twenty-eight years old. Yeah, that means I'm one of those young millennial girls. I'm still in the first half of my lifespan (at least I'm assuming so). But I've had some very interesting life experiences that can help others and I feel many individuals can relate to them. So, I'm going to share pieces of my personal story in hopes that it may speak to you or someone you know, and help them to overcome the story they are telling themselves that they aren't enough.

MY STORY

People call me Emma, but my real name is Emily. I actually decided on this "name change" when I was in 4th grade because there were too many "Emily's". I was so sick and tired of being "Emily S." and not being my OWN person and own voice because I had to share my name. When I came home and told my parents that I would no longer respond to the name they birthed me with, and shared my brand new name with them... they responded with the story that they were actually going to name me Emma from the get-go, but at the very last minute they changed it to Emily. LOW AND BEHOLD, they were human and made an enormous mistake, in which I corrected later on in life. All is well! All is well. To this day, it's a great conversation starter when I surprise people that my real name is Emily. But my first step to who I was becoming was to find my own voice and let it be heard, by I guess - changing my name.

And God said, "Let there be light!" and there was light. (Genesis 1:3)

Besides rebelling by changing my name out of the blue, I'm normally a straightedge and 'follow the rules'. I feel that this stems mostly from the fact that in first grade, I got caught cheating on a math test with my best friend. Looking back on why, I get it.

I've realized how incredibly AWFUL I am at mathematics. Seriously you guys, in high school as a sophomore I was in pre-algebra. Math is not my strength. Can anyone relate?! To this day, I actually bought an app for my phone that is helping me continue to improve my math skills. Thank the LORD for calculators!

Okay, I'm not sure how we got on math, but it's a huge part of me because I like to joke around about it. Honestly, I'm not even embarrassed anymore. God created all of you math geniuses to take that role on the world. I'll be transparent and upfront with you math guru's...I NEED YOU. See? Everyone has a purpose. Never doubt yourself.

Since the day I got caught in first grade, if I took one step off the path God paved for me, I would get in trouble. Growing up, the people around me would do all sorts of things without getting caught. It's not even that they hid it well, because they didn't. But if I decided to participate in anything that didn't align with God's plan, He reminded me that I needed to change directions and get back on the right track. I started to notice that these things didn't happen to everyone else. Almost like he chose me for something greater because each mistake I made in life, came with a big consequence. But this molded me into who I am today.

Another important thing to note about my personality is that I'm super competitive in sports and games. I get frustrated if I lose at something, but for a while I lived my life striving to be in second place, instead of first. I am extremely empathetic and passionate for other people's feelings and desires, that I never want to take the gold because the men and women I compete with have dedicated long hours and sometimes their lives in order to win. Even though I did the exact same things, I would rather see someone else elated and proud with a gold medal than myself. For a long time, I struggled with this. We are supposed to be humble, kind and selfless. I viewed winning as being selfish. And when you view winning as selfish, you will never win.

But then I started seeing some amazing Christian athletes show humbleness and grace, even on top of the podium. I started digging into the Bible about winning and came across this verse:

"Don't you realize that in a race everyone runs, but only one person gets the prize? So run to win!" (1 Corinthians 9:24)

That's totally a verse I base my life on now. Give all you have every ounce of energy - and try to win. Winning isn't selfish if you're competing in an event that's DESIGNED to have a winner. You cannot steal a win from someone unless you cheat. If you strive to win the race, your win could push the silver medalist to try harder and win the next time around. It took me 28 years to understand this.

A constant reminder to me is that God gave us all skills, abilities, and moveable limbs. He gave us lungs, a heart, and a brain. He did this because He wanted us to USE them! Use them to His GLORY! Even those that have three limbs or half limbs continue to race. Continue to strive. Continue to win. So, if we are given these abilities, we need to use them as best we can. God created our bodies special. Each one win, doesn't mean that God isn't proud of your efforts as long as you "run to win the race". So don't feel ashamed or guilty if you take second place, as long as you gave it your best. of us has different needs. We are all unique! But just because we don't win, doesn't mean that God isn't proud of your efforts as long as you "run to win the race". So don't feel ashamed or guilty if you take second place, as long as you gave it your best.

I was never the best at whatever I choose to do. Every time I became better than I thought, I would stop and search for something else I'm bad at, and try my hardest to become better at that next thing. That whole concept of not wanting to take someone else's gold medal kicked in every time I saw myself getting better.

But whenever someone whispered in my ear that I am not capable, that I don't have the genetics, skill or strength to become good at something, I wanted to show them that they were wrong. "I can do all things through Christ who strengthens me" was my first thought - every time. I love showing others that with God, I can be unstoppable.

"I know that you can do anything, and no one can stop you." (Job 42:2)

When we have thoughts in our mind that we are not capable, or someone else tells us we aren't, we have to remind ourselves that we can do anything with the help from the Holy Spirit. As long as we are doing it to glorify Him, and using our gifts in His honor.

"For I can do everything through Christ, who gives me strength."
(Philippians 4:13).

Sports and physical activity are great examples of showcasing God's unwavering power within us. When we are physically tested, we are simultaneously mentally tested as well. I was constantly tested while playing soccer in high school and college, because I had to work my tail off in order to be seen, heard, and play in the game. Extra conditioning after practice, drilling on the weekends...I always had to put in more work than others. But in the end, it was always worth it.

After my college soccer career had ended, I had to feed my competitive nature. I found CrossFit shortly thereafter and realized, I was really bad at it. In CrossFit, you have to squat. What I haven't mentioned yet is that from first grade to even now, I sprained both of my ankles A LOT. To the point where I had very limited mobility and very flimsy ligaments in there. When you have limited ankle mobility, it's extremely hard to squat below parallel.

Here we go again, time to work my way up the ladder (secretly

I loved it). At my Level-1 CrossFit certification, I was the center of attention as to "how to train a client who cannot squat properly". That was hilarious. Then, a few years later - when I thought I drastically improved my ankles, I went to get Mobility Certified and the instructor looked at me and said, "I've never seen such worse ankles in my entire time working in this field." I asked him how long he's been into fitness, he said about 20 years. Just fueling my fire. Remember when I told you that if someone told me I can't do something that I try to prove them wrong? And so my story goes on.

I would spend one hour per day, everyday, working on my mobility issues. Ankles, shoulders, upper thoracic, hips. All of it. As I did, I got better at CrossFit. I got STRONG. I was fast. I was absolutely surprising myself and surpassing where I ever thought I could be! I began to love to compete in the sport (and take second and third place). Along this journey, I started to become extremely passionate about coaching. So after I graduated college with my B.S. in Health Promotion and Wellness, I became a full-time CrossFit Trainer.

In 2015 I went on to the CrossFit Games North Central Regionals with an awesome team. I felt that I may have been the weakest link, but being the weakest link or not - I made it. That was my all-time goal. Regionals. I would spend hours upon hours training, filming myself, tweaking things, and working out. I look back now and wonder how I managed to do all of that, but wow was it FUN! I will never have the opportunity again because CrossFit has restructured the CrossFit Games, and no longer has Regionals. It was a great experience and I praise God every day for helping me to get there.

After Regionals I caught the bug. I wanted to get better, and make it with the big dogs. I had a lot of potential, but had never fully unlocked it. My mental barrier of not competing to win the gold kept getting in my way. But I trained harder than ever before and became the top 100th female in the CrossFit Games Open - North Central, and I could see the light at the end of the tunnel. My hard work was finally showing. 2016 was going to be my year.

But, God had another plan. A few months later I tore my hip labrum and was faced with a similar battle I had years before with my shoulder, but this time, I was getting married a few months later. My doctor told me that I was not supposed to walk on my leg for 6-12 weeks, which meant I was on crutches for my wedding. Can you imagine? Having to crutch down the aisle on the best day of your life? Not being able to dance or celebrate? I was faced with having to battle mentally, find patience and overcome adversity again.

"For they disciplined us for a short time as it seemed best to them, but He disciplines us for our good, that we may share His holiness. For the moment all discipline seems painful rather than pleasant, but later it yields the peaceful fruit of righteousness to those who have been trained by it." (Hebrews 12:10-11)

One of the greatest gifts God has ever given us is the ability to mentally plow through adversity and challenges. With the Holy Spirit living within us, we are able to see through obstacles and conquer them with finesse, while also staying humble.

Without batting an eye, I put on my game face and went to therapy. My game face looks scary, if you ever watch me compete. I turn into a warrior. Warrior Emma was coming out again, but God prepared me for this year before. I didn't know it yet, but he was training me to fight this one, and fight hard. I was no longer striving to be competitive in CrossFit anymore, I was striving to have my life back.

My injury happened in the Spring of 2016. I continued to coach my classes on one leg, which taught me how to become a better coach by verbalizing and cueing others to demonstrate the proper movements and technique I was looking for. I got married that summer to the love of my life, and I gripped my father's hand real tight, and walked down that aisle - crutch free.

My physical battle will continue to be ongoing. I don't think it will ever end, as I still struggle with my hip still to this day. But the miraculous thing is that my strength and skills are back to where I was prior to my hip injury. I haven't gotten surgery, just rehabbed and strengthened. I am able to compete again, and push my body to its limits - all for His glory.

"Do you believe God is powerful?
If so, then start believing you are too."

"For when I am weak, then I am strong"
(2 Corinthians 12: 9-10)

In January of 2017, I opened my very own CrossFit gym in Sussex, Wisconsin, and in June of 2018 I started my own remote training and online nutrition lifestyle coaching business.

God is using me to be a leader and set an example to others. He was teaching me how to find my voice and speak. He was training me for this chaotic path ahead, but I needed to learn how to lean into His strength and trust in His POWER before getting to this point. I've grown to see how powerful we are, when we have Christ in us, for God's power to us is His VOICE.

When I think about the word "POWER" I think about strength. With the Holy Spirit, we are incredibly strong both physically and mentally. We are capable of so much more than we give ourselves credit for, because God tells us "we can do all things through Christ who strengthens me", but for one reason or another we don't believe it wholeheartedly.

We start to let thoughts creep in that we are where we are, and that's "just how it is". We think that we aren't capable of accomplishing our dreams because we say that we don't have the talents or abilities to do so. We don't have the right credentials. But here's the thing, with the Holy Spirit, we can RISE UP to our full potential. God lives in us which proves all those other excuses and internal narratives wrong. Do you believe God is powerful? If so, then start believing you are too.

May you continue to live your life by finding His voice within you, knowing that you have a purpose, that you are unstoppable, and that with God, YOU ARE POWERFUL.

"If we were to ever uphold our power, sometimes we become worried that the people around us will feel smaller or of less value -which of course, isn't true. God has literally engrossed His own power within you to use for His plan and purpose. By not allowing yourself to utilize this wonderful gift that is POWER, you are being a disservice to yourself and those around you."

Safe

Feeling Safe In An Unsafe World

BY CARRIE REICHARTZ

Early in life, I lived through sexual abuse and other trauma where my physical, mental, and emotional safety were threatened. I never felt safe in my own skin or in any situation. I had many rituals I would do to try to give my mind the illusion of safety. If I would sleep in my full clothes, never have my back toward a door, do the right things, be perfect - the list could go on and on – then I would be SAFE. Those methods seemed to work for many years, but then bigger and uncontrollable situations arose– health problems, divorce –and my control tactics didn't work.

Overwhelmed and unable to fix, manage, and control my life's circumstances, I lost trust in my family, my friends, and myself. Having experienced a lot of pain and disappointment, now I realize that a true sense of ease does not come from where you are, who you know, or what you own. Safety comes from an abiding faith In Christ.

As a missionary who travels back and forth several times a year to Mombasa, Kenya, I get the same question all the time – "Is it safe there?!?!" I quickly answer with a question of my own, "Am I truly safe here?" As a woman in Christ, I am just as safe in a Kenyan village as I am in my suburban home. Earthly institutions like police and fire departments certainly provide a level of physical safety, but calamity can find me anywhere. I am truly safe whenever and wherever I am connected with a loving and all-knowing God.

The times I entrusted my safety to another person or partner ended very poorly – physically, emotionally, and financially. If I look to my husband for happiness and security, he will live under the burden of unrealistic expectations and eventually burn out. What's more, I will most certainly be disappointed because he can't control the world any more than I can. Today, I have an amazing husband thanks to, in large part, my faith in God to protect me.

I have also believed that taking specific courses on topics (marketing, coaching, etc.), that I would be enough. I thought I would feel confident and could start that new business or nonprofit; but if I didn't have that degree or certificate, then I wasn't enough.

Trusting that some "thing" can provide true safety and security will leave me very vulnerable. I could spend hours and hours on school work while day-to-day responsibilities were ignored. Diplomas can't truly comfort me or my kids. They'll fly away in the slightest breeze, never mind a strong storm. Additionally, all the time and money I spent on course and classes affected my kids' views of higher education. They don't want to get so deep into debt that they're paying for a degree 25 years after earning it; in a field they're no longer interested in. Accumulation of material things leaves a huge void in our lives. They provide no security or safety and instead cause more and more problems.

True safety is a mindset, not a physical circumstance. Proverbs 1:33 states "…but whoever listens to me will live in safety and be at ease, without fear of harm." God's sovereignty, His ability to control all circumstances, gives Him the ability to make us safe. Zechariah 10:12 goes further by quoting the Lord's declaration, "I will strengthen them in the LORD and in his name they will live securely."

This doesn't mean we won't have struggles. It means that even in the toughest times, if we listen, He will have our back. Through the Holy Spirit, who is in me if I accept Christ into my heart, we will be flooded with peace, calm, and rest -- If we choose it. True safety is just one thought away.

Coming to this realization freed me from the pit of depression, anxiety, and a completely fear-driven life. In Christ, I made it through a divorce, life threatening medical issues, the unexpected death of the father of my children, and major career and life changes. Trusting Him also led to building a pregnancy crisis center in Kenya, amazing friendships, a thriving women's ministry, and a million other things I cannot even begin to list. It has brought me to stable ground in a chaotic world.

Don't get me wrong, I can still misplace my trust, and the results are predictably bad. Jesus, unlike many people in our lives, does not expect perfection. When I do eventually turn back to Him, situations and circumstances become easier to act on and live through. A true test of my growth and faith is the length of time it takes me to realize that I misplaced my expectation of safety and security. How quickly do I stop and turn it over to Him?

"Trust Him. Trust Him with your present. Trust Him with your past. Trust Him with your secrets. Trust Him with your mind, heart, and soul."

Tell Him you trust him. Tell Him you accept Jesus as your Savior who rose from the dead to overcome our struggles and sin. The Holy Spirit will then be with you, and He will give you all these things. He will hold your hand, guide you, and take you into glory! (Psalm 73:23-24)

Looking back over my life, I realize the danger of seeking

a sense of safety from earthly sources. It is important to uncover where true trust lies if we want to live a full life and feel secure. Let's dig a bit deeper to identify the people, places, and things you may be entrusting your safety to, how to turn it over to God, and practically take advantage of His protection.

It's useful to actually put pen to paper for this. In one column, list who, what, and where you've designated as a Trustee for Your Safety. Next to that trustee, write why that seemed like the right solution at the time. When similar situations or circumstances come up again, you might want to consider depending on and leaning into your faith as a true source of safety, peace, and ease. Here are a few categories and examples that might get you started:

People

Myself ("Those who trust in themselves are fools, but those who walk in wisdom are kept safe," Proverbs 28:26.)

Kids

Parents

Pastor

Significant other

Spouse
Places
"Nicer" home

"Safer" neighborhood

Things

Excessive drinking / Medication not as prescribed

Food

Government agencies

Job / Promotion / Paycheck

Reputation

Stock market

TV

As you can see, no matter how hard you try, you will not find safety and security by putting trust in any person, financial avenue, ourselves, pleasing people, things or ourselves.

I can hear you through the pages already, "That all sounds great Carrie, 'Trust my safety to Jesus.' But what the heck does that mean?"

Here are some specific actions that will get you started and from there, the Lord will lead you better than any other human could: Be in the Word. The Bible has a lot to say about how to live life. Read it! Even if it doesn't make sense as you start. Be consistent. Be in the Word at least five days a week, even if it's only for a few minutes a day.

There are some great podcasts and phone apps that can get you started. If it is not making sense, take the time to paraphrase what you are reading in a notebook. That helped me a lot when I first started. Join a Bible study group to share your perspective and experience.

Meditate on the Word. Read a small part of the Bible – usually one verse. Think deeply about what it is saying. Look at every single word in that verse. Imagine how the people in and around the story felt. What does it mean in your life?

Draw from the Word. Draw or doodle an image based on your reading. It slows down the brain and allows you to think through what the verse is saying to you.

Motivate from the Word. Write scriptures on index cards and place them in busy places for you – bathroom mirrors, car dash boards, in the kitchen, wallpaper on your phone. Work on memorizing these scriptures.

Act on the Word. Do what the Word says. (James 1:22) It is not enough to simply read the Bible. We need to integrate its lessons into our daily lives. This does not happen overnight and it is not meant to. But slowly, one truth at a time, the Holy Spirit will lead and guide us on practicing these principles every day. Here are two basic examples (remember to allow the Holy Spirit to guide you): Love one another. How can I do that today? Do not covet. What can I do today to be content with myself and my surroundings?

Make a Joyful Noise. Surround yourself with Christian music.

Community Fellowship. Christian friends keep you encouraged and accountable. The key to implementing these changes into your life, one at a time, is by having community around you that you trust and who are trustworthy. You can find this in Bible study groups and Christian companions who listen, empathize, and encourage you, but also lead you back to the Word of God. Make sure what you share will stay between you and the person you share it with. Get out there and do something for someone else. If we stay focused on us and our problems, they will get bigger and bigger. As we get out in the world and help others, we will see how big God is and know He can and will take care of our problems, too.

Communicate with God. Prayer is vitally important to realizing a sense of safety in Christ. Praying is not only talking with God, but it is also listening. Prayer is not necessarily something that takes place kneeling at the foot of a bed or in a certain spot. It can be

148

done in your car as you're driving. It can be counting to five when you're in the middle of a situation with your kids. It can be writing or drawing. For me, writing keeps me more focused and creates a record to see all God has done through prayer.

"Don't limit prayer to kneeling at your bedside! Let your day be filled with time that you are communicating and listening to God!"

Using God's word and praying what the Bible says is very effective. For example, if you tend to worry, find some verses on worry in the Bible, add your name to them, and pray them regularly throughout the day. Another necessary component of prayer is humility. Admitting your need for help. Acknowledging before God that you cannot do this alone, and in so doing, asking others to pray for you. Some of prayer time should be done in silence, listening for guidance in random thoughts and feelings. Everything can be taken to God in prayer from the biggest – what should I do with my life – to the smallest – get me to my next location safely – and everything in between.

Take some time right now to put some (or all) of these practical steps on your calendar. If you are seeking Him with all your heart, you WILL see a difference in your life. You will start moving from fear and trusting in Jesus who knows all things and deserves your trust.

He will keep you safe. No one else can.

In peace I will lie down and sleep, for you alone, LORD, make me dwell in safety. Psalm 4:8

I Am Worthy

BY DEBORAH WARREN

Worthiness was as foreign to me as a flying car. It was as distant as the stars and the planets, and as unattainable as capturing the invisible wind. When my mother conceived me while on birth control, I was setup for hardship right from the beginning. It didn't help that my conception also came with violent morning sickness for her that led to vicious day sickness that ended in brutal night sickness. My mother was literally sick from the day of conception until the day I was born, so a bundle of joy I was not.

When I was born, my mother didn't think I was the cutest little thing in the world. Oh no! In my mother's eyes, I was not as physically appealing as my siblings. My skin was too dark, my lips too big, and my gums too purple. This opened a door for the spirit of rejection to come in and bring along its best friend called unworthiness.

I learned early how to avoid the spotlight, where rejection lived, in order to avoid the comparisons between myself and my siblings, where I always came out lacking. I learned early how to brace myself in the face of disappointment that became my constant companion. And, most of all, I learned that to receive any praise or accolades or rewards, I had to perform at a superior level so my mother could have bragging rights amongst her friends. If it didn't make her look good, it wasn't deemed worthy.

My siblings, however, were praised collectively and

individually whenever we went out. My brother, the oldest and the only boy, could do no wrong. He was a handsome heir and the first grandchild on my dad's side. He was the quintessential son that every father was proud to have, and every mother adored.

My oldest sister had the lightest skin tone and was known to be a beautiful person inside and out. She was pretty as a picture and loved by all.

My other sister was a living baby doll. She was petite with a head full of long hair, and although her skin tone was a little darker than the other two, she was able to pass the "brown paper bag" test and was an acceptable pecan tan, unlike myself.

I was doing good if no one said anything negative about me, and I was on cloud nine if anyone mentioned my two dimples instead of my purple gums when I smiled. My siblings seemed to bring joy to my mother, but not me.

My mom always seemed more than happy to allow all my siblings to try any kind of activity, no matter the cost. That wasn't the case with me. With me, money was always scarce and there wasn't enough to waste on something I wouldn't finish anyway, or so I was told. That became the reason for saying no to every request I made. If it couldn't be done around the house or for free, I wasn't allowed to even try it.

Understandably, I developed a works mentality early in life. Everything good I obtained had a task attached to it. I often felt like Cinderella, except, Cinderella was beautiful and married the handsome prince while I stayed stuck in the dungeon for forty-three years. I grew to believe that to get anything decent from my mom, or life in general, I had to work hard for it. That included love, admiration, approval, or any type of accolade.

In my freshman year of high school, I was invited to go to the prom. My mom said she couldn't afford to buy me a dress, but with my parents divorced by this time, I asked my dad for some help, which he agreed to. When I told my mom about this happy outcome, she was furious - A reaction I struggle to understand to this day. I am left to guess that her own insecurities and lack of self-worth were triggered when my dad was able to assist. It seemed by asking for that help, she deemed me a traitor. Her anger seemed to grow as the day of my prom grew closer and it appeared to me that she did everything in her power to sabotage that event. I remember that day very clearly.

My sister and I woke up to a longer-than-usual list of chores. In addition to cleaning the entire house and raking the yard, I also had to mow the full yard, alone. For some reason, that wasn't a task my sister and I were told to share. It was for me alone. I remember the sweat dripping down my face as I struggled to push the lawn mower over our half acre yard. It was spring in South Georgia, but someone forgot to tell the sun, which shone as if it were the middle of August. It was hotter than hot and as I continued mowing, dirt settled on top of the sweat and formed a mud pack on my skin. I finished with only an hour before the prom. No time for a long luxurious bath, makeup session, or professional hairdo. I had to do the best I could without help from a doting mother or devoted sister. This kind of situation, one in which I was alone and uncared for, was normal and seemingly what I deserved. At that point, worth was as far away as the spring sun, something I'd never get acquainted with. Another round won by rejection.

Worthy wasn't something I ever felt. None of my interactions with those closest to me ever led me to believe I was worthy. I believed what I felt, and I felt the feelings I thought were reflected back to me from others. No matter what I gave, I didn't think I got it back in return. For years, I never felt or thought a feeling of worthiness was possible because I couldn't seem to do enough to elicit a positive response from those I loved. With no positive reaction, there is no positive internal feelings, therefore no worthiness. With rejection being my root, the fruit of worthiness seemed an impossibility.

Then one day, just a year ago now, Jesus stepped in to change all of that. It was time to make all things new and Rejection's time was up. A lifetime of rejection brought me closer to God and now it was time to heal the scar tissue left behind. The Holy Trinity entered my heart and opened my mind to address my unworthiness once and for all.

God said, "If you are not worthy of love, why did I give up my one and only son and watch him get beat and die on a cross for you?"

Jesus said, "If you are not worthy, why did I hang on that cross, separated from my Father, and fight satan and every demon in hell for you?"

The Holy Spirit said, "If you are not worthy, why did I make my home in you and give you life-altering gifts and power to do miracles?"

God then explained that for me to think I was not worthy was a slap in His face, a rejection of all that Jesus had done on the cross, and a rejection of all that the Holy Spirit had given me.

Wow! That was like a bucket of ice-cold water being thrown in my face. It was enough to open my eyes and give me a clear perspective of how much I was eternally loved by God, Jesus and the Holy Spirit.

Worthy doesn't mean I'm perfectly self-assured. It means I have a heart for God and want to bring glory to His name. It means He deems me acceptable and good enough no matter what I do or don't do. Just like a hundred-dollar bill found on the ground, no matter how bruised and torn, or what I've been through, to Him, I will never lose my value. That means I'm intrinsically worthy and never have to earn it, I just have to accept it.

*"With rejection being my root, the fruit of worthiness
seemed an impossibility. Just like a hundred-dollar bill
found on the ground, no matter how bruised and torn,
or what I've been through, to Him, I will never lose my value.
I'm intrinsically worthy and never have to earn it,
I just have to accept it."*

Author Bios

Jenn Baxter is an accomplished author, speaker, and blogger based in Charlotte, North Carolina. She has been published in numerous print and online publications and appear at festivals, Christian conferences, and private engagements across the country Jen speaks on the subjects of minimalism, clean eating, healthy living and spiritual health. She appeared on HGTV's "Tiny House Big Living", is a regular guest on the NBC morning show "Charlotte Today" on WCNC-TV and has also appeared as a guest on many popular podcasts.

Chou Hallegra is a Board-Certified Christian Counselor and Certified Spiritual Life Coach committed to helping women walk closer to God and be all that they were created to be, so they can enjoy the abundant life that is theirs in Christ. Chou is a brave woman who has learned to make brokenness look beautiful through the many life challenges she faced. She now writes and speaks to inspire others to rise above their circumstances. Chou and her family live in South- Central Pennsylvania.

Email Chou at: chou@graceandhopeconsulting.com.

Angela Mager, a holistic health coach, helps women over 40 get to the root of their weight loss challenges. Her approach removes the blame and shame of the "eat less and exercise more" mentality. With specialized education in functional medicine, she understands that weight loss, especially after 40, is not that simple. Prior to becoming a coach, Angela was a registered nurse for 20 years. Witnessing many lives ruined by chronic disease inspired her determination to be a champion of empowering wellness.

Casandra Mickle is a Human Resources Generalist living in DuBois, PA. She has two adult children. She has earned a master's degree in Business Administration (MBA) and a Master's Degree in Organizational Leadership. She teaches noncredit adult continuing education classes at Penn State University. Casandra enjoys crafting of all kinds and reading Science Fiction. She was saved at the age of 7 and has been growing in the Lord for the last eight years. Casandra enjoys attending Tri County Church immensely. Her favorite verse is 2 Corinthians 12:8-10. Casandra aspires to be a professional speaker one day to help women all over the United States find strength in the Lord.

Email Casandra: **Micklemotivators@gmail.com**

Paula Millar is a retired school counselor with a zest for reaching highly challenged students. She assisted a group of elementary school children in authoring a self-published book, Higher and Higher. Her Spirit Lives On is about coping with the death of a friend. She has dabbled in writing personal blogs that find the greater meaning behind real-life situations. She loves to write with a touch of sarcasm. Paula lives with her husband in the middle of nowhere in Northern Wisconsin.

Stephanie Miller is a certified personal growth coach, writer and speaker. Her coaching ministry, Butterfly Beginnings specializes in helping individuals who are "spiritually stuck" by catalyzing change through connection with the Holy Spirit. Her blog, www.butterflygbeginnings.net seeks to encourage women and challenge them to grow closer to God and in community with each other. As an army wife, she is a bible study facilitator at PWOC, a Christian military wives ministry. When she is not chasing her dogs or toddler around, she enjoys coffee or lunch with friends, being active outdoors and baking.

Connect with her on Instagram/Facebook:
@stephaniemillercoach.

Shawnee Penkacik is an author, social media manager, and podcast host. Her website Sunshiny Thoughts along with her podcast seeks to encourage moms to know their worth in Christ. She wants moms to know that although motherhood is messy and hard, God will give them the tools to make it through. Shawnee is married to her husband Jason of twenty-two years. When she is not juggling the duties of raising their eleven children, she enjoys her morning coffee, time with her family, or reading a good book.

Learn more at sunshinythoughts.com.

Carrie Reichartz, executive Director for the I Am Enough In Christ Women's Conferences, founder and Executive Director of Infinitely More… She takes frequent mission trips to Kenya to work with people affected by trauma and pregnancy issues.

She has a true passion for children and helping people travel through trauma into triumph by inspiring them through her personal story. You can contact her and find more about her work at InfinitelyMoreLife.org, IamEnoughInChrist.com, and the Kenya work at MercysLight.org.

Heidi Renee encourages families to embrace and enjoy life's detours. She married her complete opposite and then adopted. Twice. Heidi is the author of The Road Less Traveled: A Memoir of Adoption, Special Needs, Detours, and Love. She has a heart for the special needs parent and family, and is driven to inspire, encourage, and give hope when it is needed most. The detours we take in this life can lead us to some of the grandest places we've ever known. Heidi is a Wisconsin native who now lives in Texas.

Connect with her on Instagram @heidireneewriter,
Facebook: Heidi Renee, and her website heidirenee.me.

Emma Schilter is the owner and CEO of Rising Tide Performance as well as owner & president of CrossFit Blue Moon. Emma received her Bachelor of Science in Health Promotion & Wellness at the University of Wisconsin-Stevens Point. She is a certified nutrition coach as well as a CrossFit Level 2 trainer.

Connect with Emma on Instagram @emmaschilter,
Through email at emma@risingtideperformance.com and her
websites www.risingtideperformance.com and
www.crossfitbluemoon.com.

Dawne Suehring was born and raised in a small town in Wisconsin. The eldest of five children, a sense of responsibility and nurturing seemed embedded within her from an early age. Her sense of caring served her well in her years of babysitting; as a volunteer at the local hospital; as she worked in the nursing field. Drive and perseverance were embodied in Dawne's pursuit of her education; achieving a Bachelor's degree in Biology from Clarke College and an RN degree from The Finley Hospital School of Nursing. Dawne also achieved an Advanced Practice Nurse degree in Neonatology. A Responsible mother of three, with a desire to help others less fortunate, Dawne's passion for infants and children expanded to mission work. Traveling to Kenya in 2016 was the birth of a new passion. Dawne has completed five trips to Kenya with recent trips focusing on work with pregnant teenagers and their babies. The relationships that have developed and the spiritual growth and development of her faith are among Dawne's many great BLESSINGS.

Joy Trachsel serves women at Pregnancy Solutions. By God's grace she has an opportunity to be a voice for the unborn. She has been speaking to women for over 15 years both nationally and internationally. Joy can be heard on Moody Radio – Cleveland WCRF) as part of the Pause For Prayer Team. She is the author of The Great Cover Up and hosts the Running in Flats Podcast. Joy is married to Wally and is the proud mom of 4 children and Grandma Jo to Emma, Addie and Titus.

You can get to know Joy better by visiting www.joytrachsel.com.

Carla Ward has been called to serve the Last, the Least, and the Lost, answering the instruction in Colossians 3:12 to wear the compassionate cloak of Christ. She is the Director of Changing Hope Ministry - providing residential addiction transformation for addicts and support for families of addicts. Her instruction from God has been, "Teach Them Who I Am". As a result, Carla is a speaker and active ministry volunteer in jails and prisons. She has two sons and seven grandchildren. She resides in the Chequamegon Forest where she enjoys Wisconsin lake life.

Deborah Warren is a faith-based empowerment and mindset coach currently living in the United States. Deborah's Christian faith is at the heart of everything she does, and she uses it to empower and guide her clients into a life of success in their careers and businesses. From a young age, Deborah learned that the only way to live successfully within the turmoil of this world was by leaning and depending on God. The faith foundation that was built as a result as been at the heart of her every success and she believes that is the key to any lasting success.

You can find Deborah at www.coachdeborahwarren.com, Twitter, Facebook and LinkedIn: @ coachdwarren

Tracy Loken Weber earned a Master of Science in curriculum and design and instructional technology from Bemidji State University in 2005. She has served as educator, nonprofit President/Executive Director, Author, Keynote Speaker, University Instructor, and is currently a state-wide trainer for UW-Milwaukee. In addition, she has become an advocate for foster care and adoption and has been promoting the importance of trauma-informed care in special needs children. She is currently finalizing her doctorate at Cardinal Stritch University. Tracy is married to Thomas, and is an adoptive parent to Mario, Samiyrah, and Naiyelli (as well as Charlie, the family dog).

Contact Tracy: TracyLokenWeber@gmail.com or
Twitter/LinkedIn @TracyLokenWebe

Mercy's Light
Family

Here at Infinitely More Life, we started our ministry in Mombasa, Kenya, were we started the first and only pregnancy crisis center/maternity center in Coastal Region of Kenya.

Meet Baby Z. She is a thriving 7-month baby. She is walking with assist and crawls faster than you can turn your back. She jumps in her Johnny jumper and puts EVERYTHING in her mouth. She is developmentally advanced for even US standards.

But Baby Z's life could have turned out very different. Her mom had a very tough life. She ended up pregnant, not by choice, and was kicked out of school and chased away from her house. Many young girls in this situation end up turning to abortion and Baby Z's mom thought of that to.

Thanks to our sponsors Mercy's Light Family –safe shelter, food, water, medical care, love from our staff and volunteers, trauma counseling, Spiritual counseling, general education, and vocational training are being provide for Baby Z and her mom.

Most importantly she is learning the Word of God and living by it each day in our center. Learning who she is in Christ and to live in that every day with herself and her baby.

JOIN US IN MAKING A DIFFERENCE AROUND THE WORLD!

This cannot happen without YOU! Please go TODAY and make:

Your Gift for Jesus of $29/month or $348/ year-end yearly to PROVIDE for Baby Z, her mom, and others like her. MercysLight.org or mail your donation to Infinitely More Life, P.O. Box 510376, New Berlin, WI 53151

Sponsors get access to a private group and may other privileges contact us at MercysLight.org and find out more about the benefits YOU receive as a sponsor.

YOU ARE ENOUGH IN CHRIST

DO YOU KNOW JESUS?

Thank you for attending the "I Am Enough in Christ" Online conference. It our prayer that you have been encouraged and inspired as you have heard these powerful messages from our incredible speaking team.

Maybe you have attended this conference because you were invited by a friend and you are wondering how can you have all those things we talked about that are available to us in Christ. We invite you that if you don't know who Jesus is to simply pray a special prayer and let him transform your life, just has He has our authors in these stories. Jesus wants to forgive your sins and give you NEW LIFE.

Simply pray with me:
Dear Father God, I love you. I need you. I know that I cannot do this on my own. I'm sorry for leaving you out of my life. I know that I am a sinner. I'm sorry for my sins. Sorry about the way I've lived. I want You in my life. I surrender my life to you. I receive Jesus as my Savior and my Lord. I believe He died for me. He rose from the dead. Take me as I am and make me everything You want me to be. Thank you for reminding me that I Am Enough in You. In Jesus Name, Amen

If you have prayed this prayer, we want to hear from you. Email us at infinitelymorelife@gmail.com or visit our Facebook Page at I Am Enough in Christ and let us know today. We will help you with next steps and encourage you on this journey.

Photography credit - Ben White Unsplash

Go Deeper With Jesus!
Join us for Infinitely More Life Conferences

For Bible Studies, Conference Info, and more.

Visit us online at:
InfinitelyMoreLife.org

Made in the USA
Columbia, SC
22 December 2019